THE PEOPLE'S APOCALYPSE

Edited by ARIEL GORE AND JENNY FORRESTER

This is a book about the end times: The ground we stand on will fall into the sea or God will stomp down from the sky (he's really pissed now).

We are ready.

We've prepared for this day by hoarding grain, reading scripture, raising chickens, arming ourselves against each other, and building solar ovens for the post-apocalyptic pizza party.

We are impatient.

We've tried to hasten the end with prayer and waste, environmental activism and holy wars.

We are hopeful.

We've imagined zombies and King-Kong-sized Jesus; post-civilization utopias where salmon crowd the rivers again and new vines climb to hide all the old fast-food architecture.

We are survivalists, anarchists, environmentalists, U.S. Army special ops, visionaries, poets, zinesters, and Christian fundamentalists.

We are average: According to Pew research, 41% of Americans believe Jesus Christ will return by 2050.

This is a book about personal apocalypses: When our gardens die, when all is lost, when our hearts feel ruined, we the people rise—we soften ourselves to meet the chaos. In the rubble of it all, our worst fears realized, we build some small fire and warm our hands. And as night falls, we see that the moon and stars still rise, too, with or without us, and we begin to relax.

We are waiting.

We are human.

Ariel Gore & Jenny Forrester

THE PEOPLE'S APOCALYPSE

© Jenny Forrester and Ariel Gore

PUBLISHED BY LIT STAR PRESS

FIRST EDITION, FIRST PRINTING: OCTOBER, 2012

ISBN: 978-1-62106-287-5

COVER DESIGN BY *Andrew Farris.*

INTERIOR LAYOUT BY *Andrew Farris.*

EDITED BY *Jenny Forrester & Ariel Gore*

PHOTO & ILLUSTRATION CREDITS: *Cover, pgs. 23, 121, 161:* National Archives; *Dedication:* Argus Newspaper Collection of Photographs, State Library of Victoria; *pg. 39:* Brett Milligan; *pg. 44:* Golda Dwass; *Relevations, Signs,* and *Saviors* section illustrations: Kent St. John; *pg. 89:* Chiara Forrester

PRINTED BY MALLOY

DISTRIBUTED BY MICROCOSM: WWW.MICROCOSMPUBLISHING.COM

LIT STAR PRESS

For the Children of the Future

Contributors

Special thanks to the Kickstarter Backers
Mary Brinkley • Ajit de Silva Warren Pope • Kitty Torres
Erin Edmunson • Valerie Fitzgerald • Matthew Kovens
Andy Conn • Ramon C. Vargas • Kate Dreyfus • Eileen Alden
Natalie Kilkenney • Claudia Dwass • Hedy Zimra
Evelyn Sharenov • Patience Kim Phillips • Dot Hearn • Kait Moon
Bonnie Ditlevsen • Temple Lentz • Ron Forrester

And with special thanks to Gretchen Ermer • Mitchell Lenneville
Claren Walker • Dena Rash Guzman • Matty Byloos and Carrie Seitzinger
of Smalldoggies • Robyn Johnson • Kevin Sampsell • Gabriel Blackwell
Gretchen Ermer • Kate Dreyfus • Nina Rockwell

And with humble gratitude to Kent St. John for the gorgeous artwork.

It's really too bad people only live for less-than-or-equal-to a century. We should be more like the earth. Geology not biology. Think about the awe-inspiring things we would become if only we could get a millennium or eighty under our belts. The Grand Canyon was once a sad, wet, little groove in some otherwise uneventful dirt. All these breaks in us, all these fissures and cracks and seams would grow and change and blend and become. Our imperfections could strike some future person dumb with their beauty, inventing art right there in his virgin heart.

Instead, we have our tax-shrunk C-note of a life to live and then we're done. Barely leaves time to learn how to speak, let alone say anything worthwhile. Fucking Universe.

—ROY COUGHLIN

one   **REVELATIONS**

BRING IT DOWN	*Derrick Jensen*	1
FACEBOOK UPDATE: WE ARE THE APOCALYPSE	*Tomas Moniz*	3
SAFETY	*Katie Kaput*	13
WHEN THE PLANETS ALIGNED	*Margaret Elysia Garcia*	18

two   **PLANS**

PREPAREDNESS 101	*Center for Disease Control*	25
YOU'LL NEED A BACKPACK	*Mary Travers*	29
YOU'LL NEED A SOLAR OVER	*Sarah Leamy*	31
YOU MIGHT NEED URBAN GOATS	*Brett Milligan*	36
YOU COULD USE A COB OVEN	*Golda Dwass*	41
HOW IT WILL BE	*H.A. Burton*	45
FRENCH 75: YOU'LL NEED A COCKTAIL	*Robert Duncan Gray*	51

three   **SIGNS**

SANTA FE SONGS	*Ariel Gore*	55
THE JUPITER HOTEL	*Linda Rand*	61
TSUNAMI WARNING	*Lisa Loving*	66
LOS ALAMOS LEXICON	*Margaret Foley*	75
SIGNS OF THE END	*Susan David*	79
QUEEN OF THE GIMPS	*Vickie Fernandez*	80

four   VISIONS

WHAT WE STOCKPILE — Dani Burlison — 91

THINGS I WON'T NEED ANYMORE — Sheri Simonsen — 94

CONFESSIONS OF A BORN AGAIN — Theresa Crawford — 95

CAREERS TO CONSIDER — Sheri Simonsen — 99

THE FATES AND FELIX TORO — John Rodriquez — 100

THINGS I WON'T NEED TO REMEMBER ANYMORE — Sheri Simonsen — 104

TO HELL WITH CHICKEN LITTLE — Lasara Firefox Allen — 105

TRENDING — Sheri Simonsen — 113

HAPPY ENDINGS — Kenna Lee — 114

five   CATACLYSMS

THE RUSSIANS — Kitty Torres — 123

THE PLANES — Katherine Dreyfus — 128

THE MOTORCYCLE GANG'S JACKET — Matty Byloos — 131

EROTALYPTICA — Bonnie Ditlevsen — 133

THE END TIMES PROJECT — Yasmin Elbaradie — 142

ANIMAL APOCALYPSE — Robert Duncan Gray — 158

six DEMONS

HOW WE BECOME WHAT WE BECOME	*Evelyn Sharenov*	**163**
MYPOCALYPSE	*Jeffrey Wayne*	**167**
LA FLACA	*Tod McCoy*	**170**
BIOCHEMICAL WEAPON ZOMBIE DOG DREAM	*Yu-Han Chao*	**176**
AFTER THE VERY FIRST QUIET MORNING	*Julie Mandelbaum*	**179**
SPITEFUL COMPANION	*Deb Scott*	**187**

seven SAVIORS

THE PEN	*Carrie Seitzinger*	**193**
REVOLUTION	*Mai'a Williams*	**195**
BIRDS	*Dena Rash Guzman*	**207**
GOLD MINER PSALMS	*Jenny Forrester*	**209**
VOLITION	*Colleen Rowley*	**218**
SELF AS SAVIOR	*C.*	**219**
WHEN THE SAVIORS ARE GONE	*Leslie Gore*	**223**

one **REVELATIONS**

I wouldn't mind if the consumer culture went poof! overnight because then we'd all be in the same boat and life wouldn't be so bad, mucking about with the chickens and feudalism and the like. But you know what would be absolutely horrible. The worst? ... If, as we were all down on earth wearing rags and husbanding pigs inside abandoned Baskin-Robbins franchises, I were to look up in the sky and see a jet—with just one person inside even —I'd go berserk. I'd go crazy. Either everyone slides back into the Dark Ages or no one does.

—DOUGLAS COUPLAND, *SHAMPOO PLANET*

BRING IT DOWN

Derrick Jensen

I haven't spent a lot of time preparing for the crash of civilization, primarily because my main interest isn't in making sure that I survive it, but rather in making it happen as soon as possible.

Just yesterday I heard that ladybug populations are collapsing. I'm hearing from friends nearly everywhere that insect populations are collapsing. This is in addition to the other collapses we already know about: amphibians, migratory songbirds, and on and on. Staid scientists are saying the oceans could be devoid of fish within fifty years. Given all this, my own personal survival is trivial compared to trying to stop this horrid culture from killing the planet. Every day sooner we can bring it down is a day sooner that the earth can begin to recover.

Further, it's like an environmentalist friend of mine says, that he does his activism because as things become increasingly chaotic he wants to make sure some doors remain open. What he means by that is that we cannot predict the future, but we know that if salmon are around in ten years they may be around in fifty, but if they are gone in ten they are gone forever. So the best things we can do are to a) bring down civilization as soon as possible; and b) protect wild places as much as we can.

That said, my mom and I do have a year's worth of food stored in her house. It wasn't the peak oil people who convinced us to get this: it was my sister who is a Mormon. One belief of the Mormons is that they should have at all times a year's worth of food on hand.

One more brief thing I want to say about this preparation: although I of course believe my time is better spent trying to protect the natural world than it is preparing myself personally for the crash (through which I will die anyway because of Crohn's disease) at least three or four times per week my mom and I discuss what she should do with her meager savings to protect them as the economy collapses. Should she buy gold? Should she keep cash? She hasn't yet decided whether to get gold or to get cash, but most importantly, she has already gotten a hand pump for her well, a year's worth of food, and a shotgun, and of course neighbors with whom she has relationships. But even with her, the most important thing is that she protect as much land as possible. So she feeds birds, bears, foxes, insects, plants, soil, helping to prepare them as much as possible for whatever future they will face.

FACEBOOK UPDATE: WE ARE THE APOCALYPSE

Tomas Moniz

Update 1:

My daughter is obsessed with the Hactivist group Anonymous.

"They want to shut down Facebook," she informs me, incredulous, as if it is the stupidest thing she could possibly think of doing. "I hope they know people will just go back on to MySpace or make some new one up."

I'm excited—I Google the group's YouTube cyber warning on my silver laptop, Apple logo aglow.

"We will destroy what you so love," they threaten.

I smile.

She frets.

"But why would someone want to do that?" she asks, but I know she understands why—even as she deftly slides out her Nokia Flip Phone from her skinny blue jean pocket, reading and answering a text as if it were a skill innate to human beings from birth. She slides the phone away. "Really, Dad, why?"

I shrug, already reposting Anonymous' message to my own Facebook profile page, almost oblivious to the irony.

"I mean, what the heck will we do if Facebook is gone?" She stomps away, footfalls punctuating her point like a fading ellipsis.

What will we do?

Update 2:

Ok, maybe the apocalypse is actually happening as we speak, and it looks nothing like what we imagine.

I don't believe in zombies or vampires or plagues (ok, take that back, I do believe in plagues and, man, do I love those movies about them), but I don't think the end will come through infected blood. As fun as those possibilities might be, they ain't coming to save us... or, well, destroy us.

Instead, we have global warming, not as sexy or as fun.

We have tsunamis, hurricanes, heat waves, melting polar ice caps, and an assortment of other extreme weather happenings, which cannot simply be coincidences.

We have an environmental apocalyptic catastrophe on our hands.

Today.

Right Now.

We have irrevocably altered the environment for the worse. We are the apocalypse.

So I look to polar bears and bees. They are telling us something; they are the first signs, they are evidence, they are pattern.

We are placated, distracted, encouraged to ignore the signs, to look elsewhere. Like placing the oxygen mask on ourselves first—before our children. I update my Profile to encourage people to act.

Take me for example. I am totally distracted by Updates, Event Invites, Profile Status Changes. I tell myself that I still spend time with those I love regularly, with those I consider family, even as the first thing I do in the morning isn't roll over and kiss my lover awake or snuggle in bed with my children. I check my iPhone.

Something is wrong. But it's alright because I discover that thirty-nine of my Friends changed their profile picture.

But maybe just maybe, this slow moving apocalyptic demise is a good thing. We have a chance. We have choices to make. We can be proactive; we can even prepare, fight back.

I have always supported E.L.F., A.L.F, the Black Bloc, et al, et al. But unfortunately I was unable (or unwilling) to participate when I was young because I had children. And today as I drive one daughter to chorus, another to soccer, and bail out my son's car from the tow yard, I seem completely disconnected from those forms of actions. But survival is a many-sided affair.

Update 3:

It was an estate sale that started it. A young man sat at the front door of a squat house in west Berkeley letting people into his grandmother's home. He looked broken.

The lady who lived here must have been something else.

Crafting stuff was everywhere: multi-hued skeins of yarn, cast iron pots and pans, camera equipment.

In a back room, I discovered boxes of old negatives; NAACP prints of Oakland in the '40s, large format images. I worried that nobody would buy them and they'd be tossed. These photos were history; they reflected the good old days; Oakland as Mecca, the fastest growing black population in wartime America. Jobs and money and cheap real estate everywhere.

Until postwar American racism returned with a vengeance and changed things, destroyed lives.

But then a row of books caught my eye. Twelve books in various earthen tones on rough paper. The Foxfire Series. I had no idea what they were. They clearly hadn't been touched in decades. Opening each one, I felt like I had discovered lost biblical scripture in the deserts of Jerusalem. The books contained essays on corn shucking, moonshining, hog skinning, goat milking, rattlesnake lore and legend, water collecting. Square Dancing.

That's right: How to fucking square dance.

Not since finding the zine on How to Pee Standing Up for my daughter had I been so excited. I looked around; I coveted, I hid them with my body so no one else could see them. I pushed my way to the front and tried to act nonchalant as I asked how much for the set. He could have said a hundred dollars and I would have run to the ATM.

Instead, he told me a story:

Shit those old books. Be careful. My grandma used them like they was law. Seriously. I know how to whittle because of them books. But I will say. I knew my grandma almost better than I knew my parents. Because of those books. She'd watch us grandkids. They was like twelve of us running wild. But we all listened to her. Especially after she showed us how to skin a raccoon that had died one night in her yard. After that anytime she wanted to show us something we listened. Don't know if it was cuz we was scared or cuz we was curious. Don't matter really. She was one woman you didn't wanna fuck with. What you gonna do with them?

I have no idea, I answered.

Use them, he said, use them and you can have them all for forty bucks.

I gave him fifty.

Update 4:

We started with two chicks. We built the coop. Simple really. I initially thought to YouTube instructions. But then I remembered the books; I found out on page 212 how to construct a chicken coop, and I read the directions aloud to my two daughters. We grabbed scrap wood, nails, and hammers.

But we failed.

Both chickens killed in the first year. By raccoons!

I wondered if Grandma's raccoon really just happened to have died in her yard one night. I looked for the chapter on how to kill predators.

I found it in Volume 3, page 96.

We tried again. This time we succeeded.

So now, I watch my daughter gather eggs. We have gone on to house bees. We learned how to tune a guitar. I started making beer (yummy) and tried Kombucha (even if you make it yourself it still tastes bad). I have even decided to create a cookbook journal, recording the recipes I know my kids will never want to cook on their own once they move out. Like my famous concoction: Indian Peas and Tofu. They roll their eyes and making gagging noises when I tell them I'm making it for dinner. "Hell no," they shout and reach for the cookbook, quickly flipping to the recipes they've written down.

Update 5:

An anarchist approach to the apocalypse is that the motherfucker's happening. And like a good anarchist, I build things rather than destroy, though yes destruction is sometimes creation, but my Frankenstein is the haphazard place I share with my children and my community. When we gather and cook food, when we play music and sing stupid kid songs to the children in our family, when we harvest the herbs and attempt to make lip balm, when we clean the chicken coop and place the shit in the garden, we are not just surviving, we are living.

Even if Facebook and the myriad of other technologies that distract us still pull us away too damn often. I know and my daughters know if ever it all disappears, there is another way to live.

Today, we have a gallon of water a day for each person for five days stashed under the deck. And food: we have cans of food stockpiled. So we know what we'll do when finally the cyber-apocalypse or environmental apocalypse eventually comes to our home. We'll read and stay warm by the firelight.

Of course, we'll have to teach ourselves how to make a fire first.

It's on page 192.

HOW TO BUILD A FIRE

One of the most important decisions in building a fire is choosing its location.

- Pick a location at least somewhat protected from the weather (wind, rain, etc.).

- Try to pick a location near—not next-to—a good supply

of fuel for your fire.

- Clear away any debris next-to the spot where you will build your fire.

Once you have chosen a suitable location, it's time to gather the necessary materials for building your fire.

STEP 1: Gather tinder. This is small, light, and dry material which can easily ignite. (e.g. dry leaves, dead pine needles, paper, bark shavings, cotton cloth, etc.)

STEP 2: Gather kindling. Slightly larger than tinder, kindling is fuel which take a bit more heat to ignite. (e.g. thick bark, small twigs, etc.)

STEP 3: Gather medium fuel. For example, sticks which are at least the width of two fingers. You'll only need about an armful.

STEP 4: Gather heavy fuel. One or two thigh-sized log sections would do.

STEP 5: Arrange your fuel by size near your fire's location: tinder, kindling, medium, heavy.

Once you have gathered all of your materials, you can begin building a fire. There are many ways to build a fire, I am going to provide you with only one: the pit tepee.

BUILDING A PIT TEPEE FIRE

STEP 1: Scoop out a shallow pit in the center of your well-chosen location.

STEP 2: Gently lay some tinder in the center of the pit. Fluff it up to make air space.

STEP 3: Carefully place kindling on and around your tinder. Be sure to leave an "door" open downwind (away from the wind) through which you can access the tinder.

STEP 4: Lean medium fuel in a cone-shaped "tepee" over the kindling. Still keep that "door" open.

STEP 5: Ignite the tinder through the open door. (I'll go over that next.) The tinder will light the kindling, which will light the medium fuel.

STEP 6: Add one piece of heavy fuel to the fire. Be careful not to put out the fire when you do.

STEP 7: Add more medium fuel as needed to start the heavy fuel burning.

STEP 8: Repeat steps 6 and 7 as necessary to keep the fire going.

Keeping the fire going is one thing, lighting it is the more difficult task. I kept it simple in step 5 above "Ignite the tinder," but it would be best to present you with a few options in how to actually start a fire.

- Pack matches or a lighter in a sealed plastic bag, preferably kept on you at all times.

- Strike flint and steel to create a spark to ignite tinder.

- Use friction methods to create enough heat to ignite tinder.

- Create a hot-spot on tinder using glass (especially magnifying lens) with the sun.

Fire can be used to provide warmth, cook food, boil water, signal for help, and so much more. Treat this versatile tool with the respect it deserves.

SAFETY

Katie Kaput

We dragged all of our bulk food from Oakland, leaving behind queer friends who understood transsexual queer mama me in my pink cardigan, cat-eye glasses, all-day lipstick, and pearls. We brought heavy five-gallon paint buckets of wheat for grinding into flour, oats for rolling, and beans, my kids would remind me, for farting! We brought dozens of cans of tomatoes and jam, huge quantities of dried herbs and seaweed, and ten pounds of salt. I insisted on bringing all of our plants from our balcony garden in their heavy terra cotta pots, even though we were going to be sharing a half acre of garden space with E.'s parents, because we knew that the end was near: Certainly global oil production had peaked already or would soon, and, if not, catastrophic sudden climate change was always a possibility. We might need those plants.

I was scared of having nothing to offer my children. Maybe I was already scared of my empty romantic relationship, too, but you can't store a year's worth of love, tender touches, kisses, and soulful conversation.

Food is easy, and if you have a well and a way to pump the water, that's easy, too. So I made us safe.

For a few weeks it felt that way—safe—like we'd made a good and healthy decision by leaving the city behind and coming to live in this place of old hippies and logging families, where community meetings included discussions of what kind of explosives we'd need to blow up the bridges in the area when marauding city folk (also known as my friends) came our way after the oil apocalypse made them realize they were living in a shit-filled food desert.

There was even something romantic about clearing what had been E.'s parents' early '80s back-to-the-land garden so that we could plant our own, even if they did hover a bit close shouting advice without warning. Next-door-neighbor in-laws aside, life felt idyllic. Long walks with the kids to pick blackberries. Things we were so quickly getting accomplished, too, the seeds beginning to sprout, the sourdough culture maintained and ready, the chicken coop we were building nearly ready for our twenty-six chickens. We ignored the gunshots we heard at random hours. Yes, we were moving in the right direction. We were going to be well-situated when disaster struck.

In town, however, at the first soccer practice of our son's season, everyone was looking at me, and not in that charming small town "oh, look a new woman joined our community! Let's bake her a pie!" way. These looks were familiar to me, looks I knew preceded rude comments or permanent ignored status. Looks that, when I was alone, preceded potential violence or requests to purchase sex.

Driving back home, E. said, in a whisper meant not to carry to the children over the Led Zeppelin, "I should just take Rio to his practices… I don't work on Tuesdays anyway."

"I want to come see the practices." I reached for her hand, which was resting on the stick, but she pulled it away from my touch and onto the steering wheel.

"It's not fair," she said.

I closed my eyes, hoping desperately that she meant the things that had always been unfair: The way people reacted to us as queer parents, but more specifically to me as a trans woman. But I could only hear what her mother would have said. "It's not fair to the children."

* * *

"Her name is Pomegranate, and she is beautiful!" Six-year-old Rio had found a special friend among the chicks we received in the mail. "Look at her markings; she looks like an owl!"

At age two, Robin was content with any chick who'd let him hold her; Rio began wearing Pomegranate in a makeshift sling while he walked in the woods, played at the playground, or went to the grocery store.

But having chickens was calling my survivalist theory into questions: These chickens as pets might be fine while trucks were still moving goods across the country, but what would we do when that stopped? Since getting them, I had discovered that the concentrated egg-producing portion of the chicken's 20-year life span is about two years; after that, they contribute about as much to your household's self-sufficiency as the average guinea pig.

Pomegranate survived into young adulthood before being pulled by a raccoon through chicken wire while she slept. Rio was the one who discovered her bloody feathers around the base of the chicken coop and stuck to the chicken wire.

I told myself it was an important life lesson for the kids. Death is a fact of life.

"I just want a pet that won't die so soon!" Rio cried, inconsolable.

* * *

It wasn't long before E. and I took a walk in the woods to talk about all the things that weren't working out: I didn't like living by her parents. And we were repeating all of their back-to-the-land mistakes, as city people must. I was starting to wonder if we might not fare better hoping for urban bread lines and having a manageable little garden again than trying to do everything ourselves in rural isolation.

And E. wasn't in love with me anymore. What had started when we were seventeen with a desire to start a revolutionary riot grrrl family together, finally realized when we were nineteen and Rio was born, had ended with two very different people stuck in a place that only felt safe because it was familiar: She, driven, successful, and not at all interested, it turns out, in an intimate relationship with a trans woman, and me, totally in love with homeschooling the kids, not driven in any direction likely to supply money, and still undeniably transsexual.

I cried so much on that walk, mostly for the kids; I couldn't yet feel my own feelings. I had been trying so hard to keep everyone else safe I had numbed myself completely. And yet the kids weren't safe, not from life or the apocalypse, from dead chickens, broken partnerships, or from a mother who hadn't learned to take care of herself yet.

* * *

I moved back to the big city, moved through a custody battle, a flooded basement apartment, and enough odd jobs to feel like I was living through a slow-motion societal collapse.

But E. and I find, after all the behind-the-scenes fighting, that we've done a decent job of sheltering the kids from the worst of it. We're able to keep them safe in this way: whatever we disagree about privately, we don't put them in the middle. We speak well of each other.

I know that I deserve self-love and other love. I deserve safety and risk in equal measure. Not having my kids home two nights a week is hard, but I begin to write and I fall in love with another single mama. The kids and I safely raise three chickens we rescued from certain death at a farm where they have outlived their "useful" lifespan.

I still have a closet full of whole grains and beans, but I'm not planning just to outlive all the suckers who didn't prep. A year's worth of food for me is several weeks' worth of food for my neighborhood if there's an earthquake. It's a lot of food to share if a friend loses her job and needs to feed her kids.

WHEN THE PLANETS ALIGNED

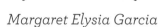

Margaret Elysia Garcia

I was in junior high on an Air Force base in West Germany the first time I heard the world was going to end. It was the '80s and I was getting off the bus and this ninth grade Hessian Iron Maiden fan says, "Hey, Margaret, don't you want to give it up to me after school—the world's gonna end tonight anyway—you wanna die a virgin?"

Say what? I was far more shocked by the revelation that the world was ending than I was shocked that he wanted in my pants. I mean, I had some Scorpions and Def Leppard at the time. I had a crimping iron. I could pass for a Hessian boy's chick.

"Dude, the planets are aligning tonight. That never happens. When it does, the world ends. Don't you read Nostradamus?"

Again, my shock lingered—the Hessian read? I hadn't read Nostradamus. I was afraid to.

By the time I got to the main doors of our two story junior high prison I thought this idea of apocalypse by planet alignment and reading Hessians might have some teeth to it. By my second period class, everybody, even Mr. Flood, our world history teacher, was talking about the world coming to an end. I took a look around the room. The white stoner Hessian was already using it as an excuse to get high and convince eighth graders to "do it" with him. Some of the R&B kids were planning end of the world parties and to kick the shit out of some girl they hated. Those of us caught between Ozzy Osbourne and Lionel Richie—well, we just sat and watched and hoped Mr. Flood would start class while we listened to punk rock and New Wave on our Walkmans.

Mr. Flood had a 1950s Dick York sort of haircut comb over and it looked like he'd stolen his wardrobe from "Bewitched." His clothes were early '60s stylish but tattered and thread bare. Most teachers at our school were the wives of officers and taught while their husbands were stationed here. But Mr. Flood was here for the long haul. He wasn't military or retired military. He'd applied to teach at Department of Defense overseas schools because he wanted to "be where the action is" and he wanted to be somewhere where he knew he wouldn't survive a nuclear holocaust. He wasn't interested in surviving.

"I suppose you all are talking about the apocalypse. That's a bunch of hogwash you know," Mr. Flood said, in lieu of taking roll. He stopped and looked at us and walked up and down a few aisles before he added, "you know it doesn't matter, right? You're in Central Europe, my friends. World War III will start here between the Soviets and us. There's no point in ducking and covering. You'll be obliterated, incinerated instantly by nuclear warheads." Some wise ass asked Flood why we were bothering to do homework then if we weren't going to reach adulthood anyhow.

Mr. Flood cleared his throat and nodded to mark the time and to have an idea of what led to our demise.

Not long after the world didn't end, Mr. Flood showed The Day After in class—just in case there were a few of us holding out for a Wizard of Oz ending in Kansas instead of the nuclear holocaust. We were in Europe, so we would die. Parts of the United States would survive, but just barely. Kansas would be fucked up and only the cockroaches were going to make it unscathed. I had the Hair soundtrack. I would go about my business of the school day humming "ripped open by metal explosions…." Comforting, to be sure.

I started thinking hard about survival, because for sure I'd be one of the few that survived; at age 13, I refused to count myself among the dead. But the recovery from the apocalypse was going to suck. You'd have to know how to do shit. All kinds of shit. Even where to put, literally, your shit. I wanted to save people, too. But I wasn't sure I wanted to start the world over with just the genes of the Hessian stoner to get us by. Every book report and project assigned in school going forward from that day was dedicated to survival research.

Sometimes people ask me how it is that I know how to make paper, soap, candles and compost. Where and why and how did I find time to learn to sew, knit, crochet, and do carpentry? Why do I have to know where all the shut off valves are? Why are my bookcases are nailed into the wall? Why do I keep my pantry stocked like a Costco explosion? In every house I have ever lived in, I map out the plan. Everyone knows the meet up location, the secret password, the rendezvous points and code words. I can pick up and leave. I can stay behind, too. But I refuse to be incinerated and obliterated.

Mr. Flood may have wanted to be toast in West Germany, The Hessian might have wanted to go out with a bang, but for whatever reason, all that head trauma of you are going to die has just made me say, fuck it. I'm living.

two PLANS

What if nobody showed up at Armageddon?

—C. R. STRAHAN

PREPAREDNESS 101: ZOMBIE APOCALYPSE
FROM THE U.S. CENTER FOR DISEASE CONTROL:
REPRINTED FROM BLOGS.CDC.GOV

Ali S. Khan for the CDC

There are all kinds of emergencies out there that we can prepare for. Take a zombie apocalypse for example. That's right, I said z-o-m-b-i-e a-p-o-c-a-l-y-p-s-e. You may laugh now, but when it happens you'll be happy you read this, and hey, maybe you'll even learn a thing or two about how to prepare for a real emergency.

A BRIEF HISTORY OF ZOMBIES

We've all seen at least one movie about flesh-eating zombies taking over (my personal favorite is *Resident Evil*), but where do zombies come from and why do they love eating brains so much? The word "zombie" comes from Haitian and New Orleans voodoo origins. Although its meaning has changed slightly over the years, it refers to a human corpse mysteriously reanimated to serve the undead. From ancient voodoo and folklore traditions, shows like *The Walking Dead* were born.

In movies, shows, and literature, zombies are often depicted as being created by an infectious virus, which is passed on via bites and contact with bodily fluids. Harvard psychiatrist Steven Scholzman wrote a (fictional) medical paper on the zombies presented in Night of the Living Dead and refers to the condition as Ataxic Neurodegenerative

Satiety Deficiency Syndrome caused by an infectious agent. "The Zombie Survival Guide" identifies the cause of zombies as a virus called solanum. Other zombie origins shown in films include radiation from a destroyed NASA Venus probe (as in *Night of the Living Dead*), as well as mutations of existing conditions such as prions, mad-cow disease, measles and rabies.

The rise of zombies in pop culture has given credence to the idea that a zombie apocalypse could happen. In such a scenario zombies would take over entire countries, roaming city streets eating anything living that got in their way. The proliferation of this idea has led many people to wonder "How do I prepare for a zombie apocalypse?"

Well, we're here to answer that question for you, and hopefully share a few tips about preparing for real emergencies too.

BETTER SAFE THAN SORRY: *Some of the supplies for your emergency kit.*

So what do you need to do before zombies...or hurricanes or pandemics for example, actually happen? First of all, you should have an emergency kit in your house. This includes things like water, food, and other supplies to get you through the first couple of days before you can locate a zombie-free refugee camp (or in the event of a natural disaster, it will buy you some time until you're able to make your way to an evacuation shelter or utility lines are restored). Below are a few items you should include in your kit; for a full list visit the CDC Emergency page.

- **Water (1 gallon per person per day)**

- **Food (stock up on non-perishable items that you eat regularly)**

- Medications (this includes prescription and non-prescription meds)

- Tools and Supplies (utility knife, duct tape, battery powered radio, etc.)

- Sanitation and Hygiene (household bleach, soap, towels, etc.)

- Clothing and Bedding (a change of clothes for each family member and blankets)

- Important documents (copies of your driver's license, passport, and birth certificate to name a few)

- First Aid supplies (although you're a goner if a zombie bites you, you can use these supplies to treat basic cuts and lacerations that you might get during a tornado or hurricane)

Once you've made your emergency kit, you should sit down with your family and come up with an emergency plan. This includes where you would go and who you would call if zombies started appearing outside your door step. You can also implement this plan if there is a flood, earthquake, or other emergency.

- Pick a meeting place for your family to regroup in case zombies invade your home...or your town evacuates because of a hurricane. Pick one place right outside your home for sudden emergencies and one place outside of your neighborhood in case you are unable to return home right away.

- **Identify your emergency contacts.** Make a list of local contacts like the police, fire department, and your local zombie response team. Also identify an out-of-state contact that you can call during an emergency to let the rest of your family know you are ok.

- **Plan your evacuation route.** When zombies are hungry they won't stop until they get food (i.e., brains), which means you need to get out of town fast! Plan where you would go and multiple routes you would take ahead of time so that the flesh eaters don't have a chance! This is also helpful when natural disasters strike and you have to take shelter fast.

NEVER FEAR—CDC IS READY: *Get a Kit, Make a Plan, Be Prepared*

If zombies did start roaming the streets, CDC would conduct an investigation much like any other disease outbreak. CDC would provide technical assistance to cities, states, or international partners dealing with a zombie infestation. This assistance might include consultation, lab testing and analysis, patient management and care, tracking of contacts, and infection control. It's likely that an investigation of this scenario would seek to accomplish several goals: determine the cause of the illness, the source of the infection/virus/toxin, learn how it is transmitted and how readily it is spread, how to break the cycle of transmission and thus prevent further cases, and how patients can best be treated. Not only would scientists be working to identify the cause and cure of the zombie outbreak, but CDC and other federal agencies would send medical teams and first responders to help those in affected areas (I will be volunteering the young nameless disease detectives for the field work).

YOU'LL NEED A BACKPACK

Mary T.

This is disaster!

Survival in the city.

No digging a trench and covering yourself with leaves.

City people need to make up a cityslicker disaster kit.

Maybe you have a disaster kit of sorts. But is the Trader Joe's Palak Paneer from four years ago still any good? Has the salt turned into a solid block? Are the Raisinetts chippable? Do you wish to share a cup of coffee with the left-behinds of little furry, albeit adorable, pests? Is the money in your disaster kit in shreds, or is it worth more than the money in your stocks? Have you raided your disaster kit so many times for camping, there's nothing left but some plastic bags? Get it up to snuff.

The Red Cross has a lovely little five-gallon bucket, chock full of enough to get you through the first day. Well, water isn't included. There is debate on whether a five-gallon can is the best way to pack your survival kit. Some folks think a knapsack would be good, but of course it needs to be protected from mice, rats, raccoons and pantry moths, the last of which will be here when we're all dead, as long as there's an absolutely unopened and totally sealed bag of brand new polenta in someone's cabinet somewhere.

Perhaps a knapsack in 40-gallon heavy plastic covered cylinder? Or a lockable truck tool box where you can also keep your tent, a Coleman lantern, your wind-up radio with cell phone recharging plugins, and your blow-up mattress?

Of course, you need some books (alas, kindles and nook books will be a loss), a couple decks of cards and a copy of "Hoyle's Rules of Games," which may turn out to a very tradable item, after you've played your umpteenth game of Canasta and need it not. It's not as if you have a job to go to. Dominoes might be good. A travel Scrabble game and a dictionary that will be the deciding source. (No "za" in that one.) How about a couple mitts and a ball? LaCrosse gear?

A musical instrument would be nice, too. Everyone likes a guitar and someone to play it.

HOW TO MAKE A SOLAR OVEN

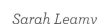

Sarah Leamy

Now let's talk about cooking off the grid. You'll need a solar oven. Sure it sounds complicated, but it's just a box. That's it. There's not much more to it than that. Oh, it's insulated. And has a glass window on the top and a door to the back on hinges. OK, maybe I need to explain myself more clearly. Solar ovens, the way I make them, are insulated wooden boxes made out of non-toxic recycled materials. I build in a door that opens up like any other oven would. With hinges along the bottom edge and slide-bolts to keep the door tightly closed when cooking. A solar oven works more like a slow cooker—at least mine does. Surprisingly, winter is the best time for cooking with these things.

In summer I bake food to a crisp and generally end up giving my concoctions to the chickens. In winter I feed myself stews, BBQ, chili, curries, and roast.

But let's get the oven built first.

I start with a window or glass pane, hopefully something about 18" x 24". More or less. Smaller means for less heat in the box. Bigger might mean you oversize the box and it doesn't gain enough heat. Something about 18" x 24" works well here in the Ortiz Mountains of New Mexico.

Next come the supplies. The window glass pane is my beginning point.

How wide and long is it? The box will be just about an inch shorter to allow some overlap of glass for rain run off. You'll also need plywood and a bunch of 2" x 2" lumber—probably six or seven pieces at eight feet in length. Don't use fiberboard or other kinds of cheaper plywood, it's full of glue and that'll be toxic with the heat generated in your solar oven. So some good plywood, thick or thin, depends on whether you plan on moving the bugger around. Heavy or light is the decision at this point. Okay, so you have plywood and lumber. You'll also need a skilsaw, drill, short screws, a couple of tubes of caulk, cardboard, aluminum foil, liquid nails, and insulation (anything from packed straw to the silver high temp insulation you get at your local home builder's store). Oh, yes, a stapler and staples, two hinges, two slide bolts, and a handle. There you go. Got that lot?

Now comes the time-consuming part—the fun part, that is—measuring and cutting and attaching the base of the oven to the four sides. Basically, I break it down in to making five rectangles out of plywood. You'll want to make the base first and measure and cut it just slightly smaller than your window. Cut the 2" x 2"s to edge the base on all four sides. Attach with the screws.

Next you can make the front of the oven. The measurement will be the width of your window, i.e. the longer side. Cut it that size by 8" for the height. You're making a box that's lower to the front and higher to the back as that helps catch the sun's heat in the slanted window. Add the 2"x 2"s to the edges on three sides but not for where it will be attached to the baseboard. See what's happening here? You're making a wooden box with the plywood being on the outside and the lumber is how you attach each side and back.

Now, work on the side panels. One edge will be 8" to match the front panel, the other far side will be 12" (the depth of your finished oven) and the length will match the base. The last side is a straight line from front to back. Repeat for the other side of the oven. You'll need to cut strips of 2" x 2" to fit along those edges now.

The next step is to get a friend to help. She needs to hold the panels upright so that you can screw the three sides to each other and make the solar box. It's beginning to look good isn't it?

The back panel is next. It'll be a piece the width of your baseboard and 12" high.

Attach with screws to the side panels. Does it look like an empty box yet? I hope so. If not, reread and then look at the finished photographs to get the idea. Try again...

The back door is a tad tricky. You'll want to cut in a rectangle shape to make an opening. I recommend cutting along the bottom edge of wherever you want to place the door. Then add two hinges on either corner for later when it'll open down and out. Mark and cut the other three sides and add two slide bolts in the upper corners to hold the door all tight and in place. Not bad eh? Looks better and better.

Insulation is next. First, get the caulk and seal all inside edges of where the panels meet and come together, smear it on to stop any air leaks. Insulation. Did I mention that yet? I use packed straw for the most non-toxic/bio-friendly solar oven, but I've also used the silver high temp insulation from the home builders' stores. Just roll it out to fit inside the panels and staple in the layers, as many as you need to fill in the gaps between the 2" x 2"s. See how it comes together now?

The goal is to use any kind of insulation that won't break down or off-gas in high temperatures. Once the insulation is flush with the strips of lumber that's holding it all together you'll want to measure the cardboard to fit over the loose straw or whatever you chose to use. Cover the shaped cardboard with aluminum for two reasons: one is to reflect the sun and focus the heat inside the oven, and it also doesn't break down over time in the sun so your insulation will last much longer. The staple gun lets you attach it without much trouble.

Time for a break yet? Hold on if you can, two more stages to go.

The oven is built and insulated. We want to put some black tin or metal on the bottom to absorb more of the sun's heat. Use high temp black paint on an unpainted metal tray or whatever you can find and cut to fit. Make sure the door still opens and closes smoothly.

Now for the window. Single pane works fine but double is better. You'll want two people to help so that one glues and one can hold it in place. Had I told you to get Liquid Nails? Well, get some and liberally cover the top edges where the window will lay on the frame you've built. Place the glass and hold it for a long time. Either that or make some way of propping the glass in place so that it doesn't slide off. It's happened to me, that sliding messy window out of control thing, so just be careful.

Take a break now.

Come back in an hour or so and tidy up, caulk any leaks around the window and door. Make sure the insulation is held in place. Check that the door closes but doesn't let out too much air. Paint the outside however you like. Make it yours.

You're good to go.

Find the sun.

Cook your dinner.

Repeat.

YOU MIGHT NEED URBAN GOATS

Brett Milligan

Derelict and abandoned spaces occur and reoccur in all urban centers as part of a city's ongoing cycles of regeneration. In the interim until such 'vacant' lots return to sanctioned uses, they give rise to spontaneous ecologies that challenge our conceptions of "natural." These landscapes contrast with the more regimented and controlled spaces that surround them. They provide surfaces for unsanctioned and creative acts; heterotopias where urban residents—human and other—find space to do things where they otherwise could not. As such, "vacant" lots are never vacant. The moment they emerge they are appropriated.

These ruderal agents are naturally suited to the post-natural conditions found in such environments; places characterized by crumbling asphalt, soil composed of demolition debris, and a latent entourage of robust 'invasives.'

Weeds are typically defined as plants growing where they're not wanted—a definition that's more complicated than it sounds. Our collective endeavors of developing cities and trading goods have intentionally and inadvertently spurred a global reshuffling of species.

Here's where the goats come in.

The contemporary domestic goat, *Capra aegagrus hircus* is a subspecies of goat believed to have been domesticated by Neolithic farmers nearly 11,000 years ago. Goats were one of the first intentionally domesticated animals, and today there are over three hundred distinct breeds dispersed throughout the world. Humans have long used goats for their milk, meat, hair, skins, and companionship. Likewise, goats have utilized human ingenuity (as applied to their bodies in selective breeding) to effectively colonize the globe. We've co-evolved and continue to benefit from one another. The use of goats to intentionally clear land is a relatively new application and the optimal workings of the practice are still being refined.

The benefits?

1. **Less fossil fuel usage. The EPA estimates that 5% of U.S. air pollution is caused by mowers. A traditional gas-powered lawn mower produces as much air pollution as 43 new cars, each being driven 12,000 miles. I'm not sure exactly how that pencils out for a two-acre lot using industrial-sized mowers, but surely it is significant. Goats keep the place mowed with zero emissions.**

2. **Slowed regeneration of weeds via digestion, rather than dispersal. The living processes of a goat's large, four-chambered stomach can digest most weed seeds, rendering them inert. In contrast, mechanical mowers broadcast seeds and often encourage weed growth.**

3. **The building of soil.** Goat droppings are a great source of fertilizer and organic matter. It enriches and accelerates organic complexity in degraded urban soils and, if repeated over time, can facilitate the nurturing of second stage vegetation. Richer soils create future opportunities to grow other things.

4. **Neighborhood love.** In addition to the 'green' branding of such practices, people tend to be attracted to biotic mowers rather than repelled by them. In short, folks like goats.

5. **Hardly any bureaucratic red tape.** Under Portland code (and the codes of many other cities), goats are considered livestock along with fowl, horses, mules, burros, asses, cattle, sheep, llamas, emus, ostriches, rabbits, swine, or other farm animals and thus are exempt from special provisions or permits as long as their use and occupation of an urban site is temporary.

The Urban Pastoral: Building Community from the Void

Bringing goats to a very urbanized location in Portland was an embodied experiment. From a community perspective, the ephemeral event activated a field of activity in the area. Neighbors appreciated the addition, with some hoping we could find a way to keep the goats there indefinitely. The longer the goats were there, the more people took on a sense of ownership, protection, and investment in the herd. The basis of the experiment—the 'work' of cutting down weeds— had morphed into the vagaries and intangibles of creating urban pleasure. People got out of their cars and paused to watch the pairing

This two-acre lot in central Portland has remained undeveloped for nearly a decade. During that time, a unique meadow ecology has spontaneously laid claim to its surface.

To conform to city regulations, the owners of this property periodically level the field with mowers. As an alternative to this practice, a herd of goats were added to the site to consume the vegetation.

During the three-and-a-half weeks that the goats were working in the field, the site became a neighborhood attraction. Rather than being a noisy and dusty nuisance, the installation demonstrated the potential of landscape maintenance to be a regenerative public amenity

Passer-by pulling weeds from the sidewalk to feed to the goats

of seemingly incongruous landscapes: A pastoral meadow with the occasional sounds of bleating goats surrounded by industrial-zoned buildings and the hum of arterial streets. Passers-by eagerly pulled weeds out of the cracks in the sidewalk to feed them to the goats (or in a generous, yet potentially problematic gesture, offered their dinner leftovers and garden scraps). People I spoke with said they never noticed or really saw this two-acre field until the goats were there. Psychologically, the lot had been a cognitive void. The goats, for their part, appeared to relish their lifestyle of roaming around to ever-new pastures.

Taking it to the Future

Could this urban ecology be taken further and made more integral to the contemporary post-metropolis? Beyond the isolated, trucked-in insertion of goats, could a city embrace continuously migrating herds of ruminants and their attendant shepherds? Roving levelers? A living infrastructure migrating from one feral urban prairie to another? A biotic replacement for the incessant hum of lawnmowers and annoying leaf blowers? Might we see a new breed of appropriately anachronistic, post peak-oil nomadic shepherds guided by open-source iphone urban agrarian apps. as they move through the city with their loppy-eared flock in tow, nutrifying disused urban lots whilst procuring milk and a bit of cashmere?

Why not?

YOU COULD USE A COB OVEN

Golda Dwass

It all started about ten years ago when my husband mumbled some-thing to me about building a Japanese wood-burning kiln into the hillside on the back of our property. Stephen has many ideas for projects and I tend to ignore most of them.

The kiln is a copy of a historical Japanese Anagama, sometimes called a tube kiln. The kiln is dug into the side of the earth four feet deep, twenty-four feet long and eight feet wide. Ten thousand bricks were used to build the kiln. A wonderful community of people has come together because of this kiln, which has been fired two to four times a year. The kiln holds a thousand pieces and uses six cords of wood to fire it. The temperature can get up to 2400 degrees.

One of the books we used was *Build Your Own Earth Oven* by Kiko Denzer. Books are useful, but it still takes an experimental and adventurous can-do attitude to build your own. Stephen's a potter and his attitude is that he can do anything without any book —how different is it than building a kiln?

Noel, our cob-expert friend, suggests a particular cob mixture for the kiln and Stephen rents a cement mixing machine. We built ours over a Labor Day weekend.

So this is how it happened:

Stephen decides that we're going to make a cob pizza oven, too. We've got the cob ingredients and, more importantly, the big mixer. We invite some friends over to help.

Stephen makes a modified cob mixture. He wants something plastic and easy to mold. Here's what he comes up with:

- **10 gallons sieved local dirt—which we collected from all of the damn mole hills around the property**

- **10 gallons fire clay from a masonry supply place**

- **10 gallons rice hulls from the agricultural supply store**

- **5 gallons short, chopped straw**

- **5 gallons sand**

- **5 gallons water**

We put all of this into the gas-powered mixer, but we could have spread a tarp on level ground, sprayed water on it, and started treading until the mixture looked like workable clay.

We build the bottom of the oven with cement blocks that form a perimeter, and we fill that in with loose rubble—basically chunks of bricks and dirt. We then put in a layer of leveling sand and then a layer of firebrick two and a half inches thick. Finally, we add a layer of cob two inches thick and we smooth that out.

We let the oven dry out for about a month and then we were almost ready to have our inaugural pizza party.

Before the party, we had to start a kindling flame at the bottom of the hearth and keep that going for three or four hours. We then put the door in the opening of the oven and placed a slab on top of the chimney. This allowed the oven to heat-soak overnight. We repeated this process for three days in a row, allowing the kindling fire to burn for several hours each day. The point was to drive all the moisture out of the cob before the real heating and cooking started.

To test for temperature, we sprinkled some cornmeal on the pizza stone. If the corn meal combusted immediately, we knew the temperature was too hot and the oven had to be allowed to cool down. Fifteen minutes later, we tested again and when the corn meal no longer scorched, we knew it is safe to start baking our pizza.

It took a few pizzas to get the temperature right, but soon we were baking each in just a few minutes. We'd set up a large table people took turns making pizzas—we even had a gluten-free crust option.

All in all, this is a great way to make something delicious and off the grid with friends. We have something to cook in when the power companies fail.

We're ready for the apocalypse.

Next project might be a cob guesthouse.

HOW IT WILL BE

⚜ ················· ⚜

H.A. Burton

H.A. Burton is a U.S. Army officer with seventeen years of experience in special operations, infantry, and engineering. He has taught Military Urban Operations and winter survival to Soldiers deploying to Iraq and Afghanistan, as well as foreign militaries, and is certified by the Federal Emergency Management Agency in the National Incident Management system and Incident Command. He lives with his wife and two kids in Portland Oregon.

The federal government in the United States manages disasters by region. In concept, it's a simple "neighbor helping neighbor" approach. In the event of a disaster affecting one geographical region, nearby regions render aid. This system works well in isolated events located in small geographical areas. Federal governmental resources are relatively limited. An ambulance can haul two to three patients at the most at any one time, and most counties have one ambulance per 10,000 people. Ambulance drivers, EMTs, paramedics, and fire fighters are often volunteers from the local community.

So, what happens in the event of a large scale terrorist attack or natural disaster? The government calls out the National Guard. The National Guard—a force also made up of volunteers and local citizen soldiers—is commanded by the state officials, and brings with it manpower and transportation assets, as well as limited medical capabilities.

 Many people know the story from hurricane Katrina—when Walmart came through with bottled water while the federal government still struggled to get an understanding of the size and scope of damage. This is still an example of "neighbor helping neighbor" model. Walmart was able to shift resources from one central logistical supply outlet and redirect it using nearby transportation resources. But what would have happened if all of the Walmart drivers were sick? What would have happened if the central Walmart supply center had been shut down?

STAY PUT OR MOVE OUT?

If you're an urban dweller living in a house or high-rise apartment, you'll likely be faced with one decision: STAY or MOVE out. When the services you're used to shut down, garbage collects on the streets, the water shuts down (or worse, is contaminated because the workers don't show up at the water sanitation center), when the pizza delivery man is dead, things in the city won't look so hot, and you won't give a damn about the night life. Being able to walk to work and reduce your carbon foot print will be the last thing on your mind.

Have a plan—this decision point is critical. If you decide to move out to the country, to try and make your way to greener pasture you need to throw away your romantic notions of living off the land, growing your own food, and taking from nature. You have to know yourself, know your skills, and you have to know your limits. Do you know how to farm, do you know how to navigate in the wilderness, have you ever lived off the land, skinned an animal for food, cooked, built a fire, and identified edible plants? Few people can be dropped in the wood with a pocket knife and make it on their own.

STAYING PUT: THINGS TO KNOW

If you decide to stay put, there are some things you need to know.

Field sanitation is critical knowledge for anyone in any situation. If you have ever used a public restroom and seen someone walk out without washing their hands then you know that not everyone understands sanitation or how infectious disease spreads. And there's more to field sanitation then just washing your hands. If you decide to hold up in your urban house or apartment, the city sanitation system may shut down. You must engineer a means of removing both your body waste and food waste from your immediate living area.

Food and water storage, acquisition, maintenance, and rationing is a critical issue and may impact your decision to move out or stay put. Keep in mind that the average human can carry about five days of food on limited rations and only about two days of water. Even in a stationary urban household, the average family of four, rationed to 1,000 calories a day, will only be able to safely store about six months worth of food and water. Learning how to safely collect rainwater from rooftops, locate safe drinking water from the ground, and safely purify and store it for use is another critical skill.

Shelter in an urban battlefield becomes your security. The ability to maintain your house, secure it from intrusion, and keep it sanitary will impact your survivability and overall physical and mental health. It's likely that as resources become scarce, those without resources will want to take from those that have resources. Thought should be given to securing windows and doors, blocking unused entry points and creating look out stations. Keep in mind that things like interior doors, closet doors, cabinet doors, and bathroom doors can be used as barriers to windows and used to reinforce exterior doors.

Fuel will become a necessity if electrical services and gas lines shut down or become damaged. You'll need to burn wood to provide heat, warm and cook food, and to make water potable. For most city dwellers, wood is scarce. If interior doors or painted wood is burned, consider exposure to the fumes given off from burning wood treatments or paint.

MOVING OUT

When you run out of fuel, run out of food, can't collect enough water, and ultimately decide to move out, there are a few things you should know. First, walking isn't fun. Walking day in and day out is tiring, puts a strain on your feet, knees, and back, and greatly reduces your sense of security and control.

Tips on movement. Moving at night can give you increased security from observation from other people interested in taking what resources you might have. In a bleak and barren future this might be a sad truth. Movement at night also may help in warmer parts of the world where it is too hot during the day, and will decrease your need for water. Moving at night has its drawbacks, and should not be tried in the wilderness unless you are skilled at night time navigation.

Load capacities. As mentioned previously, the human body can carry only so much. Humans have been known to carry up to 80% of their body weight for several days at a time with little rest, but few can do that without great physical conditioning. Most people in average shape can carry about 30% of their body weight comfortably for seven days.

Alternate routes and alternate modes. If you decide to move out by foot or by car, you may have to take alternate routes due to traffic congestion, damaged road conditions, or other unforeseen issues. You may have to abandon vehicles and take to foot, or be able to search for fuel sources to sustain your vehicle. Have a route picked out, backup routes, and back ups to your back up plan.

PSYCHOLOGY OF FEAR

The biggest threat in any emergent situation is fear. Combat fear through knowledge. People fear the unknown. The first time a person flies on a plane they may wish the pilot would keep it low near the trees, but the seasoned pilot knows altitude is your friend; it buys you time in an emergency.

Know that group dynamics will change. History has proven this through wars, civil unrest, plagues, and famines. Fear and lack of knowledge can change "the norm" and cause people to change. The battle for resources changes how people act, and changes the normal boundaries of what is right and wrong. Consider what the single mother will do when she watches the last case of bottled water disappear off the Walmart shelf or what the father do when he sees his wife and children taken deathly ill.

THE BOTTOM LINE

Have a plan, gain knowledge, learn to survive. Put aside the romantic ideas and get a gut check. Prepare yourself through education—study the plight and lives of war refugees, the stories of hurricane victims, and read about the lives of monks and clergy that witnessed the massive slaughter caused by the black death, and the Spanish influenza and other catastrophes, natural and human-caused.

The past provides of insight into what to expect in the future. Human behavior is predictable—the future is the past.

FRENCH 75: YOU'LL NEED A COCKTAIL

Robert Duncan Gray

A truly wonderful cocktail made from Gin, Champagne, lemon juice and sugar. It is said to have such a kick that it compares to being shot multiple times by a very large gun. A French 75mm howitzer gun or *Canon de 75 modèle 1897*. When the shit goes down, if I'm not drinking a French 75, I will be disappointed.

Ingredients:

- **2 oz. Gin**

- **2 tsp. superfine sugar**

- **1 oz. lemon juice**

- **Brut Champagne or other dry sparkling wine**

Preparation: Combine Gin, sugar, and lemon juice in a cocktail shaker filled with ice. Shake vigorously and strain into an iced highball or collins glass. Fill with Champagne. Garnish with a twist of lemon.

Personally, I recommend adding more Gin, as this is likely to be the most important day of your life.

three **SIGNS**

I sat in the dark and thought: There's no big apocalypse. Just an endless procession of little ones.

—NEIL GAIMAN, SIGNAL TO NOISE

SANTA FE SONGS

Ariel Gore

#1

I came to Santa Fe because my mother was dying. She wanted to die here.

We bought her a big comfortable bed and we summoned hospice.

And then my mother just stopped dying.

It's a good and expansive thing to do, to stop dying.

But then you have to think of something else to do.

#2

I started bleeding a lot when we got here. Nose bleeds, ear bleeds.

I hadn't been particularly accident-prone in my coastal city, but in Santa Fe I cut my fingers, stubbed my toes.

"Be careful," my poet friend warned me. "The desert wants your blood. I'll live here all my life, but I don't want to die here. I don't want to be buried here. Not in the desert. The star beings are waiting."

I nodded like I understood. All the connections.

The barista at the café just shrugged. "Oh, yeah," she said, "the bleeding." Star tattoos encircled her neck. "The only way to stop the bleeding is to harvest an elk."

"An elk?"

"Yeah. You eat the organs. Raw." She pushed my hemp milk latte across the counter. "I mean, if you want to stay here, and not bleed."

#3

When we were still a day out of town, in Kingman, Arizona, I checked Craigslist for housing. I found a listing for a quaint little adobe on Canyon Road, called the landlord.

He said sure, come look, but when we pulled up—me and the dogs and the kid and the trailer we were dragging, well, that landlord came running out into the street. "Do you know where you are?" he squeak-screamed. "This is the center of the art trade in all of America. This is the Wall Street of Santa Fe!"

I didn't quite know what he meant, except that we wouldn't be renting any quaint little adobe.

The landlord was white like me but he called after us: "I am one of the premiere Native art dealers in the world!" And he shook his creepy wooden doll at us like a warning.

#4

Last week we went to the occupy Santa Fe general assembly meeting, but they told us our proposed action was perhaps a bit too radical.

Couldn't we consider something more business-friendly? Something more police-friendly?

 We wouldn't want the revolution to disrupt the tourist economy.

 And, no, you cannot use the word "occupy" without permission from general assembly. Haven't you heard about the movement to trademark the movement?

Santa Fe, it seems, is already occupied.

#5

I took my son, Maxi to, to an installation, a giant post-apocalyptic pirate ship in the desert.

That night I dreamed we were on the ship's deck when a giant UFO appeared in the sky. It sent down a round beam of light. In that spotlight, Maxito danced. He liked the attention, but all the sudden he's getting beamed up and I'm rushing to grab him, and I'm too late, always too late, rushing.

Were these the star people?

No one else on that crowded cocktail-party ship deck seems concerned.

In the dream, I wondered what it was like, really, to get abducted by star people. Maybe it wasn't so bad. Maybe Maxito would have fun up there.

But then I noticed these tiny round grandmothers—Maxito's grandmothers even though I'd never seen them in waking life—and they had him, and they were sneaking him into this little wooden fishing boat to take him away. And I realized they'd staged the whole UFO thing in the first place, a distraction so they could whisk him off in their boat.

Shifty little hags.

#6

"That's what I'm talking about," the poet whispers when I run into her in front of the mustard table at the farmer's market. "The star beings. They don't want us here."

"Do you think we should move?" I ask.

"No," she says. "They don't mind if we visit. If we live here. But they don't want us to die here. They don't want to deal with our coastal spirits when we pass. You understand?" She looks around, taking in the market. "I hope you're not trying to buy dinner-makings here," she says. "They want three dollars for a potato."

#7

I'm raising chickens for the apocalypse. Like everybody. I figure even if they want three dollars for a potato, we'll always have eggs.

"I don't think that's sustainable," my neighbor says. She wears turquoise beads and a purple cowboy hat. "The hawks'll get 'em. Have you thought about an underground bunker?"

I don't know if she means the bunker for the chickens or for me and Maxito, but I think maybe my poet friend has it right. Better not to bury ourselves here.

#8

When I was a kid in California, the hippies hoarded water, brown rice, and honey wine. "For when the shit hits the fan, man."

The Christians had basements full of canned peaches, dried apples, pickled ham. Waiting for the rapture.

We didn't hoard anything at our house. We just took swimming lessons every summer. We knew California was going to fall off into the sea. At least we wouldn't drown.

And that house where we didn't hoard anything—the old craftsman my stepfather's father built—I outlived it. The new owners bulldozed the thing to build a mansion made of glass.

I managed to salvage the old wooden door and the fireplace mantle in the chaos. I have them stashed under a freeway outside San Francisco. If I ever get out of Santa Fe, that'll be my bunker.

#9

We're on Canyon Road, first Friday. We're shopping for authenticity, but I still can't stop the bleeding.

"I'm going to have to ask you to leave," the woman at the gallery says to me. She has blue eyes like mine and almost enough pale makeup to cover her freckles. "Leave, now, please," she says—this increasing urgency. She covers her mouth with her hand. "Please," she says. "You're going to get blood on the native arts."

#10

I almost killed myself this morning, swerving to avoid a rattlesnake on an unnumbered country road.

But when I looked in the rearview, I realized it was already dead.

THE JUPITER HOTEL

Linda Rand

The spring flowers burst open too soon and the bloated dumpsters around the Jupiter Hotel smelled too ripe because of the unseasonal and sudden heat. Oregon was beginning to feel more like California. People walked around in tank tops. It was weird. But it was fun, too. We left our doors open for air and music always proclaimed a party. Musicians loved to stay at the Jupiter Hotel because it was attached to the Doug Fir where they were most likely playing a gig. I was there on my insurance company's dime after the house fire that killed my cat, Pluto.

Jupiter, planet of expansion. For a time at the hotel I did feel my world grow generous. I met a young jazz musician who crooned so sweetly to me. In a soft smooth voice, "Baby, you're so sexy," and I could hear a drum brush drag in my mind's ear. "Can I look at your body?" His blue eyes were like quick fingers flying around black and white keys. Sometimes we wouldn't close the blinds of our second story window. Sometimes we'd romp around so much the whole mattress would slide off and we'd laugh and right it.

After a late gig he'd knock on my door, looking ridiculously handsome, cufflinks twinkling in the little blue domes that lit the hotel at night. Sometimes we walked around downtown, the night sky cut with gleaming sky scrapers. In the morning he'd rest his head on my chest or in the hollow of my waist and then when I wasn't expecting it, he told me he loved me.

I stared at him, stricken. I don't think he ever said it again.

The perfect day is the perfect expenditure in refining exactly who I am, no more and no less. No lies, no grudges, nothing unsaid, nothing owed. This is my preparation for when it all ends. I don't like to buy more than I need, make more than I need. A stuffed fridge doesn't look nurturing to me but like disorder and probable waste. There's an art to perfect balance, to run out right before replenishment, to have perfect flow.

I ran into an old friend when I was buying art supplies for a commission and we decide to walk up the street to Noble Rot and have a nice glass of red. We're four floors up on the balcony with a picturesque view of the bridges and river but the air is heavy with a greenish cloud cover. Rhett says he doesn't like it.

"It's weird. I don't trust it."

"It's unusual," I agree. We're both from Hollywood and familiar with all the visual blooms of smog. My favorite were the lavender night skies in summertime, redolent with the smell of eucalyptus.

"To dying well," he lifts his glass.

"What?"

"I feel like my life is to learn to die well."

I tell my lover this later, when we're in bed, and he thinks it very strange.

"Your friend seems intense," his cool blue eyes consider me, "you're both pretty intense."

I had loved to hear him talk about work, jargon so different than the visual realm where I lived. Sonic environments, charts, and of course his jokes.

"Q: How do you get a musician to bitch? A: You give him a gig."

I turned to him, adjusting the rumpled bed sheet, "I know I've asked before, but for some reason I haven't quite understood. I even looked up tonic on the computer."

He had used "melody in the tonic" during some conversation early in our relationship and it captured my imagination, seemed like a poem. Now he said something dry and for some reason just as un-illuminating. I was usually so adept at finding some fanciful handle to understand things obscure to my field of knowledge.

"There's nothing deep about it," he said.

For the first time I could feel our expiration date.

Why do I breakdown completely before I breakthrough? It's like every cell in my body has to assimilate the new instructions for a life that will extinguish a part of me while giving birth to me that doesn't exist yet. It's like breaking into a new atmosphere, jarring and burning away all that is superfluous. Anguish is my meteor mind.

We switch off the lights and as I listen to him breathing quietly I slip into a dream where I'm walking around in my cold dark house. No renovation is visible. I hear my dad's voice calling me from the basement and I carefully creep down the metal steps.

"Dad?" I feel a sad dread.

"Little Linda, sweet poor Linda."

Sitting in a high backed mahogany chair is a man sized black cat and my sleepy dream logic tells me it is my dead father's hair and my dead cat's whiskers melded into one during the fire. They are one. My oracle, my totem of love. He bursts into flame.

In the morning my lover washes his face in the little slate tiled bathroom, puts his glasses on and talks about buying ribbon mics. He's starting a recording business and loves buying equipment. He loves shopping in general. Acquiring things.

After he leaves, I get some coffee in the lobby and Heather, the front desk clerk says, "It's so disturbing all the radiation from that Japan quake, and all those birds dying. Did you hear about that?"

"Yeah," I pause, stirring some honey into my coffee, thinking of all the bees and their mysterious disappearing act, "It's like the universe giving birth and it's a difficult one. Like an enormous evolutionary cosmic upheaval."

"Did you hear about the mass extinctions?" her kohl lined blue eyes very wide.

I think about everyone I have ever loved.

"The oceans." she explained. "The coral reefs. It's much worse than anyone thought."

Suddenly I feel untethered; free. The earth is displeased and we are now going.

TSUNAMI WARNING

Lisa Loving

I work at a newspaper where it's part of my job to post all the Associated Press stories and video about tornadoes, hurricanes, mudslides, earthquakes, oil spills, and wide-scale bombing runs by US forces. So I've watched funnel clouds converging on a commuter bridge in Boston during rush hour, I've interviewed people who saw Mt. St. Helens erupt and then drove in to work. I've lain in bed in the middle of the night, forty weeks pregnant, lurching side to side through long tremors and aftershocks—then rolled over and gone back to sleep.

See? Sometimes you're just wrong—Well, kids, looks like the apocalypse only came to Southwest Washington this time—and sometimes you're just too preoccupied to care. One day maybe it'll be the real thing. At least no one will say there weren't any warning signs.

Travel Journal: Fukuoka, Japan, 1997
My husband, Leaping Louie Lichtenstein, The Most Explosive Lithuanian Jewish Cowboy Juggler Ever to Come Out of Northeast Portland, had scored the vaudeville equivalent of the lottery: a gig in Japan. He'd perform for three weeks in the luxurious shopping mall at Canal City at the southernmost tip of the islands.

Me and our two kids James, five, and Lela, four, scored the vaudeville family equivalent of The Lottery: We got to go too. Leapin Louie went first; me and the kids followed a week later. After a twelve-hour flight with a stopover in Helsinki where I screwed up my exchange rates and accidentally bought a foreign newspaper for $26, the kids and I arrived in Fukuoka and settled into the perkalicious deluxe hi-rise hotel room.

While Leapin Louie cracked whips in front of the Kentucky Fried Chicken in the Canal City shopping mall, me and the kids took the high-speed ferry from a dock near Fukuoka Tower to Marine World Uminonakamichi.

It was a dark and stormy morning. There was a current of electricity in the air. A purple, gusty rain blanketed the neighborhood as the Fukuoka Tower'—studded with radio receivers and power sources—rose in a Frankensteiny magenta neon glow in the center.

Marine World Uminonakamichi, a seashell-shaped complex built on a peninsula jutting into the Pacific, is probably the coolest aquarium in the whole world. Maybe too cool, because James and Lela ran full speed from Aqua Live Show to Happy Sea Otter Meal Time to Marine Science Lab to Snack Bar to Gift Shop. We'd seen it all before noon.

It rained like a cow pissing on a flat rock. We got back on the high-speed ferry and stepped off onto the dock into water four inches deep. "You know what? Let's go find a cab back to the hotel," I said.

We hydroplaned off the dock and onto the boardwalk. We reached the street just as a lone taxi swallowed an expensive woman in ruined white stiletto heels; the water was deep enough to splash a little into the open cab door. The door slammed and the car fishtailed off, spraying a six-foot fountain of water on either side and leaving us stranded.

James and Lela held tight to their inflated dolphins on sticks. They looked up at me. Water whirled around them. I grabbed them both by the hand; the water was at their knees. It was clear like ocean water, with playful little waves and eddies.

No sense panicking in front of the children. "Wow," I said. "Isn't this exciting? Why don't we just go ahead and walk home instead of taking a cab?"

"Why, Mama?"

"Well, I mean, we'd miss all this fresh air and exercise if we took a taxi."

"Mama," Lela said. "What are you talking about?"

"Um, let's just go."

It was getting dark. I didn't have a watch, but it couldn't have been later than 3:30 p.m. Fukuoka Tower was easy to follow—covered with mirrors and lights, it shimmered against the angry purple sky.

A row of shiny storefronts spread across its base. We washed up into a gift shop. We stood for a moment looking out at the storm. "Anybody have to pee?"

Lela laughed. "That's funny, Mama. Who wants to pee in the rain?"

Unfortunately I could see her point. "Ahem, we're about eight blocks from the Hi-Rise Hotel De Luxe, but I don't see any buses or cabs. "We should just walk."

"You mean, swim, Mama," Lela said. "Geddit? Swim?" Ha ha.

I bought us each a new umbrella, the deep, bell-shaped kind you can pull down over your head and see everything through the plastic in the color the umbrella is. In about one second I realized I'd have to return my own umbrella because I'd have to physically hold these kids through whatever the hell was going on out there.

We plunged back in. One block. Two blocks. The water was about twelve inches deep and still clear; the storm didn't seem scary, really. It was easy to navigate because the westernmost district of Fukuoka has a lot of weird tall buildings, like Fukuoka Tower and even a Fukuoka Dome. Three blocks. Four blocks. James repeated the same question every three minutes: "How many blocks, Mama?"

Lela smiled and splashed. "It's like the biggest founting in the world," she said.

"Fountain," I said.

"Founting," she said.

At the halfway point, we made visual contact with the Hi-Rise Hotel De Luxe. As I looked at it in to the distance, I imagined I could see our window. In my mind's eye, I saw inside the fridge. It was empty. There were no beers or cookies. My head ached. There was no aspirin. No dinner. I looked down at the kids. Water that was now just below my knees hit them halfway up the thigh.

Up the street the water had swollen but it wasn't really flowing. I could see a grocery store about a block and a half away. Yes, on the way to the Hi-Rise, thank you very much. Score another one for the team.

"Uh, yeah, we need to go to the grocery store," I said.

"What?" James said. "Go to the grocery store? Mama, isn't this a flood?"

Objective: Don't panic the children. "No, uhm, no, this may look like a flood, but really it's just a bit floody. Seen any cars floating down the street yet?"

James' eyes flew open. He gasped. Great.

"The grocery store is on the way, anyway. We can get chocolate milk."

We kept to the sidewalk. Soon it started an uphill slant, and the water receded. Now it was back down below my knee level; thigh level for the kids. At half a block to go, we fast-splashed up the parking lot and in the door.

We stood just inside for a moment, dripping like we just went scuba-diving in our clothes. We left a dripping trail from Pain Relievers to Alcohol to Dairy Case, Candy, and Meat Counter. This sort of thing must happen all the time, I thought. In fact, all the other people looked perfectly dry, perfectly normal.

Then again, we were too by the time we made it to the checkout. A grocery store wall clock showed 4:00 p.m. Through the big glass windows it looked deeper but also less dark outside.

We lingered a little longer on the island that was the grocery store. I plotted the shortest route to the hotel. We'd have to cross the street. You could see from here the street was deeper than the sidewalk.

"Okay, kids, this is going to be tough, but the team is tough!" I hitched our four new plastic grocery bags, two over each of my wrists, then grabbed one kid with each hand.

And it was deeper, past thigh level on Lela, and she was no longer amused. I tugged the kids down the sidewalk as fast as I could. I thought: Okay, I'm scared now. I really wished my mind would start wandering.

"Let's play Remember Fun Festivals," I said. "Remember that festival in Belgium where it was so hot we all got sunburned, and we saw that giant horse circus? Remember the big sausage-cooking pits, and the farmers in their white smocks, and the sausages were all sizzly and drippy, and the farmer-guys gave them to us on bread rolls, right with their bare hands?" Both kids looked up at me with smiles in their eyes, but not on their mouths. My hands gripped theirs so hard, I was already losing circulation, but they didn't complain.

I said, "Of all the shows, ever, what shows do you guys like best?" Water ran into my mouth while I talked. It was like swimming.

"I like Uncle Bobarino's show, when he puts the wheelbarrow on his chin and juggles on the rolla bolla," James said. "I like the Australian guys that dressed like fish and played vacuum cleaner horns and followed people around." He gulped a mouthful of rainwater. The water was two feet deep now, past his thigh.

"What about you, Lela?"

Her face was stoic as she trudged on the scariest path of all—she was a little bitty thing, now waist-deep. She looked up at me, teeth clenched, dragging herself forward with an effort.

"I really like Venus, Goddess of the Diabolo's show," I chattered. "I like her two electric diabolo tricks."

"I like ... I like ..." Lela squeaked. "I like Uncle Rudy and Cosmo and Guapo and Stinky Monkey," she said.

"I remember the first time I saw the Payasos, and Uncle Rudy wore his bald-head wig and he rode a horse puppet, and he jumped over a flaming banana," I said.

Lela smiled into the storm. "And... the fairy-dressed people... way up in the sky... and they did acrobax."

"Acrobatics," I said.

"Acrobax," she said.

We dragged forward a block, then one more block, and a block-wide eddy of water hit us from a side street. It pulled us into the intersection. Suddenly Lela and James both were submerged chest-deep. They grabbed at me simultaneously, almost knocking me into the swirl with my hands weighted like stones by the grocery bags. We clawed our way back onto the sidewalk, where the water was back to thigh-high. We were just across from the Hi-Rise Hotel De Luxe. We still had to cross the street.

As rain pounded, I could feel my eyes filling up with water hotter than all the water around it. I looked down at the kids; the bottoms of their inflatable dolphin sticks were underwater.

"Objective," I said. "Don't panic!" My nose let out a big wet snarf. "Okay, we've really got to hurry if we want to eat those Chips Ahoy cookies while they're still fresh." I looked down; all the grocery bags were partially filled with water now, and the Chips Ahoy cookies were completely submerged. For the last time, we pushed off into the wet unknown. I called out: "Chips, ahoy!" Bracing against the tide, we were ready for it this time—it was deep, but we moved forward.

I couldn't see the curb. The kids were rain-whipped and the street river tried to drag them out of my grip. I wondered if we were really going to make it. I thought of the Mad Magazine version of "The Poseidon Adventure," the scene where Shelly Winters, guest starring as a former Olympic swimmer, must swim underwater a long distance to save everybody's lives. Except that Shelly Winters was goddess proportioned, clearly not suited to a long distance underwater rescue, and everybody knew she would die in this attempt. They had a cruel laugh at Shelly

Winters. God, I thought, please don't let me end up in Mad Magazine. And don't let my last thoughts on this earth be about Shelly Winters.

Then suddenly my feet hit a curb and I almost went down again. I looked up—it was the curb of the Hi-Rise Hotel Deluxe. Like wet mice we climbed out of the water and up the red-carpeted entrance. Employees saw us coming and opened the door, then followed behind us with mops all the way to the marble elevator. Up in the room I saw the time: 4:15. We could have been killed out there, and the whole thing took only fifteen minutes?

 "Mama," James said. "Can we watch TV?"

THE LOS ALAMOS LEXICON

Margaret Foley

Growing up in the '70s and '80s, I worried about the mushroom-shaped nuclear bang. We lived in Los Alamos, after all, where Little Boy and Fat Man, the two nuclear devices used to bomb Japan in World War II, were developed during the Manhattan Project. The ensuing Cold War ensured the town's own form of job security; but it was a security based on designing and maintaining weapons—on political insecurity.

Most days, being a child in Los Alamos was no different than being a child anywhere else. Sometimes I got along with my two younger sisters, and sometimes I didn't. I was in Brownies and 4-H. I went trick-or-treating for UNICEF. I went to camp in the beautiful Jemez Mountains. But there were a few twists. In Los Alamos, we thought Z for Zachariah, a young adult novel about a teenage girl who survives a nuclear war, was non-fiction. In Los Alamos, if a teacher unexpectedly quit, any number of parents could pinch hit as the advanced chemistry or physics teacher. In Los Alamos, our first ATM machines were called ATOM Tellers. One of our many canyons was known as Acid Canyon because of hazardous waste that had been dumped in it—signs along the edges warned Danger High Explosives.

As kids, we discussed nuclear politics on the playground. If the Soviet Union attacked Los Alamos, would those mono-brow, fur-hat wearing leaders flatten the town to destroy its scientific genius or would it force the scientists to work towards its evil plan to conquer the world through a series of rigid Five-Year Plans? While there was no straightforward answer to this apocalyptic question, if push came to shove (which it often did on the playground), we all felt, deep down in our hearts, that the American Way would triumph.

In Los Alamos, nuclear weapons seemed normal. Summers home from college and grad school, we all took jobs at Los Alamos National Laboratory. In Los Alamos, we had a local language that underscored the town's unusual culture while simultaneously making that culture seen perfectly normal.

It's been more than twenty years since I left Los Alamos, but whenever I hear certain words and phrases, I remember where I'm from.

The Lab. No matter how many labs you spend time in—from school chemistry labs to crime labs—if you're from Los Alamos, there is only one lab—The Lab, always spoken in capital letters. In daily conversation, nobody ever refers to it by its official name, Los Alamos National Laboratory. It is only The Lab, as in: The Lab is helping ensure the reliability and safety of the nation's nuclear weapons. That's good to know. If we're going to have nuclear weapons, they should be safe and reliable.

The Hill. This is a nickname for Los Alamos, which technically isn't located on a hill, but atop five mesas separated by deep canyons. The Hill is also always spoken of in capital letters. The idea of a city on a hill recalls that Biblical phrase that a city on a hill can't be hidden, and when that city has developed the atomic bomb, that's certainly the case. When you live on The Hill, every once in a while, you like to "go off The Hill." It can be claustrophobic to live where everybody knows everybody. Problem is, everybody who lives on The Hill likes to go off The Hill to the same places, so you can never really get away. No matter where you go, there you are.

Salvage. This is not some fabulous reclaimed wood for an eco-chic Atomic City remodel. The Lab's old salvage yard was an Aladdin's Cave where you could purchase decommissioned Lab property. My father once built a telescope with metal scrap from the salvage yard, a telescope I later used for a science fair project where I charted sunspots for a month. Trinity. I guess when most people hear the word Trinity, they think of the Father, the Son, and the Holy Ghost. In Los Alamos, it's the name of a street, Trinity Dr., and it has historical, not religious, resonance. In Los Alamos, the street name refers to the Trinity test, which took place near Alamogordo, New Mexico on July 16, 1945. It was a test to see whether or not the nuclear bomb designed by The Lab scientists would actually explode. It did.

Badge. Los Alamos is full of badges—the police have badges, of course, the town's doctors have hospital badges, FBI agents have badges, but the people who work at The Lab have the real badges. Lab badges are a status symbol. If you had a security clearance, you had a badge with a blue background, and if you didn't have a security clearance, your had a badge with an orange background. There were other levels of badges, too. I once worked at The Lab translating Russian documents, which I then gave to someone with a higher level badge, who took them to do something I couldn't know about. Clearance. The Lab and the government need to minimize any potential repeats of the Klaus Fuchs incident—he worked on the Manhattan Project but passed some of its secrets on to the Soviet Union. A big no-no. To get a clearance, the FBI investigates your background for a few months or a year. Agents talk to your friends and neighbors, who usually call you to let you know they've been questioned and to find out where at The Lab you'll be working once you get your clearance. When I got my security clearance in college, our across-the-street neighbors, who'd known me since I was six, told my parents they'd been asked about me and had assured their interlocutors that I was wonderful. The achieving of the security clearance meant I were now a full-fledged member of The Lab, could go behind the gate, and could indulge in a little black humor by telling people without clearances that I'd like to be able to tell them what I do, but then have to kill them.

Behind the Gate. This refers to the areas of The Lab you must have a security clearance to enter. To get behind the gate, you must have a blue badge. Every classified area of The Lab has a guard station, and you must always show your badge to the guard when entering and leaving the area. Once I was exiting a building in a bit of a hurry and forgot to show my badge. The guard smirked: "If you take one more step, I could shoot you."

SIGNS OF THE END

Susan Davis

On the day the bulls ran in Newport, I was home with pink eye.

My best friend, a dentist, sat in the laundry with four down comforters cycling on high.

The window shattered and there he stood, a green washcloth and a bra

hanging from his left horn.

It seemed symbolic, with tsunamis and earthquakes and rumors of war,

and she a Catholic.

Our generation may be self-absorbed, but eschatology is not lost on us.

She said the bull stood there, smelling like Clorox and salt wind, snorting at her through his nose ring, kayakers in riot behind.

I feel like that sometime: people staring, a lime in my hand, having forgotten

what needs zesting.

QUEEN OF THE GIMPS

Vickie Fernandez

"But Cecelia what if the sky starts falling down and I'm at my house?" I squeeze Cecelia's limp hand, our shoulders grazing.

"Just run over here, Luz. You know your mom will be too busy crying about the end of the world to notice that you're gone." Cecelia's breath is like steam on my cheek.

"But how will we know it's really the end and not just a warning like the first time?" I whisper, fear making echoes of my words.

"Trust me, you'll know." Cecelia smiles, her teeth like broken windows—sporadic and jagged.

The whole thing started one afternoon when we were playing house on Cecelia's concrete stoop. She insisted on being the dad every time, tucking her feathery hair into her father's fedora and yelling, "Lucy, I home."

She'd hold me too close, arms encircling my waist as she pressed her half-opened mouth to mine. I'd flutter my lashes and cry "Oh, Rrrrrricky!"

We were feeding our baby dolls mock spaghetti and meatballs when the sun disappeared and the sky turned the color of a used coffee filter. A neon vein of lightning crackled through the clouds and thunder rolled. Before we could gather up our toys, we were being pelted by unidentifiable objects. Cecelia and I ran inside, our dolls abandoned on the pavement.

Through the split in her mother's gauzy drapes, we watched as bits of what could only be pieces of sky came crashing down.

"Mommy," Cecilia screamed.

"Ay, que pasa, niña?" Cecelia's mom pushed through the beaded curtain that separated the kitchen from the living room. She was a thick woman, her hair Brillo-Pad coarse from too many perms. She wore gold-plated rings on every finger, bracelets that jingled when she walked.

"What is that?" Cecilia pointed to the raucous sky.

Cecilia's mother peeked out the window and made the sign of the cross.

"Dat? Oh, dat is a warning from Dios." She picked at a scab on her arm, a dark glimmer in her eyes. "It means that el fin del mundo is coming. Ju be careful because one day, if ju no good, dee whole sky will go PRACKATA!" She lunged towards us, clapping her hands. "And it will fall on ju head." She laughed.

Cecilia and I looked at each other, terror and excitement buzzing between us.

I'm not sure whose idea it was but from then on, every day after school and on weekends, Cecilia and I lay face up under the cheap iron frame of her mother's queen size bed—the box spring precariously close to our faces. We wanted to see how long we could lie still in that confined space without moving.

"If the sky falls down then the house will get smooshed, right?"

"Umm hmm." I spread cheese onto a rectangular cracker with a little red stick.

"If we hide under here, we'll have the mattress to protect us, because everything will bounce off of it. Then when everything is done and all the bad people are dead, we can crawl out and God and Jesus will take us up to Heaven, because you know, we're little and pure and stuff."

I nodded and handed Cecelia the last cheese-smeared cracker and checked our time on the red stopwatch we borrowed from her brother Miguel's room. It had only been thirty minutes and I had to pee. Our longest running time was three hours and forty-five minutes. We would've made it to four if Cecilia hadn't had one of her convulsions.

Cecilia didn't like to be treated like there was anything wrong with her. She made fun of her withered limbs just to prove that point.

We incorporated "gimp" into our vernacular, after gloriously stumbling upon it while looking up dirty words in the dictionary. Looking up words was one of the things we did under the bed.

"Gimp sounds much better than cripple or invalid. Right?"

"I think so. It sounds like you should be in the circus or something." I squinted at the giant dictionary propped on my stomach.

"I want you to call me the Gimp from now on, actually no, call me Cecelia Queen of the Gimps. Okay, Luz?"

"Yeah, that sounds cool. Hey, Queen of the Gimps, do you know what gonads are?"

"No, what?"

"Balls."

We laughed, rolling back and forth on our backs like capsized turtles.

The accident had left Cecelia's entire right side paralyzed. Standing still, she looked like any normal, lanky kid but when she walked, her limbs lagged behind her, torpid and bloodless. Occasionally, Cecilia's dead side would twitch, confused and eager to feel. Her good side, overwrought with the weight of her frame, would protest and she'd have to stand up and walk it off.

The accident happened one night when Cecelia's brother and his friends were playing a game called el muerto. The premise was to lie in the middle of the street, eyes closed and body stiff, and pretend to be a corpse. Whoever held out the longest, when an oncoming car approached, before rolling over, had the biggest cojones.

Once the kids had their fill with dare deviling, they sat on the stoop sucking on ice pops and trash talking. When no one was looking, Cecilia crept down off the stoop and lay in the street, arms across her chest, stiff as a board. She would have walked away unscathed if the drunk driver hadn't swerved into a parked car just as Cecilia went to roll away from his tires.

Everyone on the stoop jumped to their feet, startled by the sound of colliding metal. It wasn't until she started to scream that the boys noticed Cecilia in the middle of the road, seemingly intact. As they approached her tiny body, they realized her right arm and leg were crushed.

She had the biggest cojones of them all.

It's been two months and we've started to stockpile supplies in a small corner at the foot of the bed. So far, we had two gallons of water in milk jugs, a bag of Doritos, ten stiff pieces of Bazooka gum and a flashlight.

I'm sing-whispering, "I want a Coooool Rider" from our favorite movie, "Grease 2" and staring at the stopwatch. We're just about to beat our record when Cecilia pulls down her pants and starts feeling around, her face taut, like she's looking for something. Then she stiffens and a deep wet sigh escapes her mouth. I stop singing, frozen.

Cecelia turns to me, sweat glistening above her lips, her mouth a fleshy pit.

"Now it's your turn." She says.

I shake my head, glad she can't see how red my face must be under the cover of our dark hiding place.

"It feels really good. I can do it for you if you want. My brother,

Miguel, does it to me sometimes and it feels even better that way. It's called singando. But you can't tell anybody. It's a secret, you know, like how we hide under here."

"Umm…I don't really feel like it," I say. Thinking this is something you don't do in front of your friends or your brother.

"Maybe we should go back to practicing for the end of the world just in case."

"Whatever." Cecilia pulls up her little white shorts.

Before Cecilia told me about her brother touching her, being at her house made me happy. I'm an only child, never left alone, always surrounded by doting adults. At Cecelia's, it was like we were invisible and free to do anything we wanted.

I insist we spend more time outside and away from Miguel who has started to follow us around the house instead of hanging out with his friends. He pushes his greasy hair away from his acne-covered forehead and just stares at Cecelia.

School is over and summer stretches before us, long and uncharted. We're standing in Cecelia's yard picking the poison berries that grow red and firm in the thick green bush along the fence between our houses. Cecelia's mother warned us, "Ju never eat dose because ju will die."

"I'm starving." Cecilia says rubbing her belly that peeks out from under her T-shirt.

"I have two dollars. I can buy you a snow cone when the ice cream truck drives by."

"Nope, I'm hungry right now," she says and pops a handful of berries into her mouth.

"What...why...what are you doing? Spit them out!"

Cecelia grabs her throat with both hands and falls to the ground with a thud.

"Cecilia," I cry, pounding on her chest with my fists.

She flails for a moment and then stops moving all together.

It's not until I start to cry that she sits up and spits the berries, red and wet onto the grass.

"Got you," she screeches.

"That wasn't funny. I thought you were dead!"

"Luz, it was a joke. Why do you have to be such a cry baby?"

"I'm not a cry baby. You're just mean and I don't like your dumb, stupid games."

"Fine, I guess, I'll just have to find a new best friend."

"Nobody's going to be your friend because you're a ..."

"I'm a what? Say it. Just say it, Luz. Because I'm a gimp?" The word sounds charmless now, full of spit and malice.

"No…I didn't mean."

"Whatever. Get out of here. I never want to see you. Never ever again."

I stand up, shake the dirt from my knees and walk home. Through hot tears under my breath I huff, "gimp, gimp, gimp!"

That summer I spend time in other yards and houses with different kids. We do fun things like play hide and seek and Candyland. I miss Cecilia but revel in the lightness of doing carefree things. I don't miss her brother's greasy face and dirty hands. I don't miss spending hours hiding under that bed with dust bunnies in my hair, afraid that Cecelia is going to pull down her pants and shake herself loose in front of me.

It's been weeks since I'd even thought about Cecelia or the end of the world. Then one afternoon, I'm loading up my Barbie Camaro with GI Joe action figures and I hear the eerie sound I'd heard that day at Cecelia's. I run to the window, my heart thumping and my legs ready to run the forty-seven steps to Cecelia's front door, up the steps and under the bed with the dust bunnies.

"Mommy, mommy, mommy," I yell.

"Que pasa, mi amor?" Mom kneels down and places her hand on my shoulders.

"The sky is falling. It's the...it's the...end of the world. Hurry, we have to hide under the bed."

Mom's mouth slacks in to a puzzled grin and she hoists me up in her arms. "Honey that isn't the sky. It's hail."

"Hell?" I start to cry.

"No, not hell...hail. It's just frozen water." She carries me to the front door and turns the knob.

"No, mommy, nooooo!" I wrap my arms and legs around her and wail.

She forges ahead out the door and onto the porch where she holds out her arm. "See, baby." She hands me a fist full of grainy round ice.

She's right. It isn't sky, just teeny tiny snowballs.

I climb out of mom's arms emboldened by this new knowledge. When I stick my hand out, the hail stings my palm. I look over at Cecilia's house thinking she must be hiding under the bed. I feel a tugging in my chest, a pity for her and her sad, sordid life of hiding and secret touches. That's when I see her. Twirling around in the middle of the street, a tornado of marmalade flesh, head tilted back, mouth open wide, catching what she must think is sky on the tip of her tongue—not a care in the godforsaken world.

four VISIONS

We caught a rattlesnake / Now we got something for dinner . . .
There was a shopping mall / Now it's all covered with flowers . . .
If this is paradise / I wish I had a lawnmower . . .
I miss the honkey tonks, / Dairy Queens and 7-Elevens . . .

—TALKING HEADS, *NOTHING BUT FLOWERS*

WHAT WE STOCKPILE

Dani Burlison

My mother grows worried as she questions me. "Do you know where I can get one of those outdoor ovens? You know, like the ones those women in India use?"

Now in her early seventies, she dishes out concerns, plans her life and limited income around the possibility of impending crisis. Convinced The End is near, she takes steps to prepare herself for a life of mayhem. She stocks up on nonperishable food items; organic canned beans and vegetables, instant dried soup mixes and other various mystery edibles from the local grocery outlet. She stores plastic jugs of water in the shed behind her tired trailer in the sweltering north end of California's Sacramento Valley. Back issues of O Magazine and Utne Reader lay across towers of books bursting with tips and alarming information about everything from homemade healing remedies to government conspiracies.

Some people call this hoarding, but my mother's just covering her bases. The outdoor oven will come in handy when the government collapses and when all of the world's oil is depleted. The water will be for drinking and cooking, naturally. And who knows? Maybe the books and self-help magazines will serve as kindling if the pages of informational tidbits don't bring the spiritual enlightenment they promise.

I chuckle at the shift in my mother's world view, but I only have myself to blame for fueling her paranoia with the introduction of Democracy Now! and various AK Press publications. And maybe her ideas of a planet-wide catastrophic future resembling "Children of Men" aren't entirely far-fetched.

The world is changing. Rapidly.

My small town childhood taught me about hunting, fishing, growing and canning food. My uber-leftist education at San Francisco's now defunct New College of California trained me to conduct direct action, taught me about the complexities of watersheds, solar power, wild food sources, and natural healing remedies. I raise chickens, can plant a permaculture garden, and concoct herbal remedies. I can even make minor repairs to my bike, build cob structures and gut fish. My emergency kit includes grapefruit seed extract to purify water, a bottle of potassium iodide in the event of nuclear fallout, an LED flashlight, some band-aids, and a solar cell phone charger. Still, when it comes down to worst-case scenarios, I'm afraid I'll fail miserably.

My internalized sexism tells me I'll never survive the apocalypse without a man.

Something also tells me I'll be lucky to survive it without guns. My daughters and I remain armed with only homemade bows, a couple of old, dull pocketknives, and a squirt bottle used to keep cats out of houseplants.

Aside from gathering and utilizing practical day-to-day necessities, there's another important factor to consider. The apocalypse isn't merely about natural and man-made disasters rendering our electronic devices and economic institutions useless. Nor is it strictly limited to events resulting from global warming and the peak oil scare. The apocalypse holds the promising gold nugget of spiritual enlightenment, or what I like to call a shift in consciousness.

Fundamentalists believe Jesus Christ may personally send gorgeous invitations in gold set calligraphy and one-way first class tickets to Never-Never Land, leaving the rest of us to burn in an eternal abyss. I like to think they're wrong. I believe the shift in consciousness is already underway, rolling and surging through the streets of London, Oakland, Gaza, and Cairo. This shift may be charging forth from communities no longer able to shoulder the pain and oppression they've endured for years, decades—even centuries. The shift might begin in socially unacceptable ways, with fires and looting and damage to private and public property. Regardless, they—we—are rising up in various and crucial ways.

This shift is a forced one, and it's gaining momentum.

In a perfectly idealistic apocalypse, communities will come together to grow food, build homes and educate children. We'll revive the lost art of story-telling and practice hand sewing textiles around fires while bottles of plum wine ferment in salvaged storage buildings. We'll be more confident in our strengths, contributing our own unique talents, which we'll unearth while corporate America falls to its feet and the looting and riots are over.

And hopefully, we won't need guns.

A three-hour drive from my mother's stockpile, my house sits in a quiet little neighborhood directly on the San Andreas fault line. I try to be as prepared as one can be with an unpredictable and jumpy fault line calling the shots. For now, my plans are fluid, changing with the ever-changing world.

THINGS I WON'T NEED ANYMORE

Sheri Simonsen

- **Printer ink**

- **Season tickets**

- **Vacuum bags**

- **Calendar**

- **Job interview clothes**

- **Good credit**

- **The gym**

CONFESSIONS OF A BORN AGAIN

Theresa Crawford

A s I parented my daughters, I tried to prepare them to lead lives of quiet Christian desperation, just like me. It was the only life I'd known.

I didn't yet know that the version of Christianity that I was trying so desperately to believe in was a uniquely American, Westernized, Colonialized version of a religion that was basically Eastern. I didn't yet know that it had been edited and re-edited over the centuries by mostly white, powerful men who just wanted to try to keep people in line. I found this out much later.

So here I was, a young mom who'd been raised Catholic, who'd been swayed to become Baptist by my older sister. I read devotional books every morning, like Stormie O'Martian's The Power Of a Praying Parent. I prayed through this book, even after The Power of a Praying Wife failed dismally to save my marriage. So, even though God didn't save my marriage as my church lady friends promised he would, I continued to believe. I had, after all, prayed that if I was meant to stay married, I could stay sane, too. When I was obviously losing it, driving my husband's Audi three blocks away to search it for evidence of infidelity, I took it as a sign from God that it was O.K. to divorce him.

"Lord make a way where there is no way."

Now that I was parenting alone, I figured I needed all the help I could get. Didn't all the media talk about how dire it was for children to be raised by a single parent? Just more evidence of our country's slippery slide toward Armageddon. The Power Of a Praying Parent seemed to cover all the bases—it was a formula for success. If I just followed the prayers in the book, my children would be prepared for anything— totally protected and in God's hands. How cool! What parent doesn't want her children to be totally protected by the Big Guy in charge? The first prayer is Becoming a Praying Parent. Good, I was already doing something right.

The second prayer is Releasing My Child Into God's Hands, followed by Securing Protection From Harm. But how do we release our children into God's hands? What exactly does it mean? How does this not just become rhetoric? I really wanted to know, but to enter into this kind of thinking requires a sort of non-thinking—we live in a universe of energy and matter, and not even the church ladies I talked to had seen God's Hands. So this was an existential premise I had to latch onto. And I either threw my kids in the wrong direction, or God totally missed the catch, because my children didn't end up in God's hands, nor was I able to secure any amount of protection from harm that I could directly attribute to God.

Still, I was a single mom. According to most, the world was going to hell in a hand basket no thanks to my kind. So I kept praying. The prayers went on, Feeling Loved and Accepted, and Establishing an Eternal Future. They were things any good parent would wish for their kids. Of course I wanted an eternal future for my girls.

When the rapture happened, when all the good people were called back to God, I wanted us all to be sucked up into heaven together. Some days I really hoped the rapture would happen sooner rather than later, because amidst all the talk of God really looking out for us, I was beginning to wonder. How could I make sense of the kidnapping, rape and murder of a friend's niece? They were good Christian folk, too. Did this mother just not pray hard enough for her daughter's protection?

As my girls reached their teen years, there were long stretches when they didn't feel loved and accepted by me or anyone else—let alone a God in the heaven. There were years of wondering, and questions, and even anger. My youngest finally said, "Either God is an asshole or there's no such thing."

I was scared. When I asked her what she meant, she said, "Mom, I became Baptized and then you and Dad got divorced. I tried to pray and be happy, and then I was diagnosed with depression. Then we found out the depression was caused by hypothyroid disease. If God's in control, He's an asshole."

I wasn't prepared for this, nor for finding out, soon after, that the youth minister at our church was raping girls, and that our church elders, who in their wisdom wouldn't allow women to be elders, never did a background check on him.

My daughters' response: "Mom, aren't you glad we didn't want to go to youth group?"

My response to them: "Yes, and so glad my power didn't extend to making you go."

I had to come to terms with the fact that I couldn't prepare my girls for life, or for the Rapture, just by praying. I was outraged.

While I was a born-again Christian, I was admonished not to feel (or express) anger. I've found this echoed in the culture at large. The message is simple: Anger is un-lady like and will earn you the label of bitch. But the youth pastor's crimes were too violent to ignore, and my anger too strong not to listen to. I wrote the senior pastor a letter (which was never acknowledged), and left the church.

When I was ready to give up my dependence on a deity, I found a strength in myself I didn't know existed. I found strength in finding out who I am, and why I thought I needed a deity, or someone like Stormie, to show me The Way. I've found a lot of answers lately. I'm learning more and more to connect with and listen to my emotions, letting them lead me on the way to make good decisions and keep myself and my family relatively safe.

Listening to my anger and acting wisely on the information has created the space for me to grow. Unlike Stormie, I find the only way to live or be ready for the end of the world as we know it is to be informed by my feelings, and to express my anger. My daughters were able to do this, and I could learn from them. Internalizing the anger only made us depressed.

As we prepare for the future, whichever way we're heading, we need to be connected to our own inner warriors. I pray now that my daughters walk in wisdom, feel their feelings, defend their right to be angry, and understand the religious and cultural attempts to circumvent their authentic joy. The rest is in their hands.

CAREERS TO CONSIDER

Sheri Simonsen

- **Midwife**

- **Trapper**

- **Carpenter**

- **Blacksmith**

- **Musician**

- **Storyteller**

THE FATES AND FELIX TORO

John Rodriquez

M om says throw out the garbage. She usually takes it out herself in the morning but she's mad so she tells me to take it out now, Sunday night. She's mad because I didn't want to eat my bacalao. She says it's because I ate a half a pack of Chips Ahoy so I lost my appetite. But if I'd been hungry I would have eaten. I told her I probably would have eaten if I was hungry but it still would have tasted nasty. So now I'm throwing out the garbage.

The elevator's not working so I'm dragging the Hefty bag down the stairwell and Mr. and Mrs. Walcott and Kissie and Shelesa are coming up the stairs. I stop and say hello. Mr. and Mrs. Walcott say hello and keep walking. They smell like McDonald's. Kissie passes me and sticks out her tongue. I had McDonald's and you didn't, she says, That's why I have a yo-yo and you don't.

She's right.

Shelesa is behind her with a yo-yo, too. You can play with mine, she says.

But I don't know how to use a yo-yo. She says that's okay, she'll show me how. Then she screams up the stairs Mom, can I play out front with Felix?

Did you finish all your homework, her father asks even though she was talking to her mom. Almost, Shelesa calls back. Finish your schoolwork first then you can play out front.

Shelesa tells me that she'll finish her homework and then she'll come down and play yo-yo with me even though I heard her dad. She gives me her yo-yo and tells me to practice for when she comes down so we can play. Then she runs up.

I try the yo-yo. It's not working. I figure I need a lot of practice so I yo-yo while going down the stairs with the garbage. Halfway down a flight of stairs I trip. Instead of falling on my face like last time I float down real soft and real slow like my mom and dad are carrying me only my mom can't lift me because I'm big and my dad can't lift me because I don't have a dad.

I'm standing on the landing and someone's ruffling my hair. I don't like it but I can't tell anybody because I don't see anybody. Then I see three ladies dressed in white and the stairwell full of clouds. The lady ruffling my hair has shiny hair like a new penny. She's got big breasts like the woman on the cover of the magazine Jose showed me in the lunchroom only the lady in the magazine had gloves on and no dress and this lady has a dress and no gloves.

She says, You're going to come with us. We'll make you the hero of the new age.

I say I have to throw the garbage out or my mom'll get mad.

Wouldn't you rather stay with us?

I think about it and then I say no.

Then the other lady with the yellow hair like Joyce's necklaces says, But if you come with us we will make you smart and brave and rich and your mother will be very proud of you. Come along.

Will I have to eat bacalao?

No.

Will I have to take out the garbage?

No.

Okay.

Then the lady with silver hair like a tin can says Well done, but now you must leave all your belongings here.

I let go of the garbage bag. Then since they don't say anything I push it a little away with my foot, but then they still stare at me.

Everything, she says, from your glasses to your sneakers. You are to begin again, Felix, so everything you possess must remain here.

I try taking off my glasses and the yo-yo hits the frame and makes a plasticky noise. I can't go with you, I say.

Why not? all three ladies say.

I don't know who to answer so I take turns looking at each lady.

I can't leave the yo-yo on the staircase. It's my friend's. I told her I'm gonna play with her when she finishes her homework. So I can't go with you.

That is unacceptable, the lady with the can hair says. You have been chosen. No one refuses the call.

Shelesa's my friend, and it's her yo-yo. She let me borrow it to practice for when she comes downstairs so we can play, so I can't go with you. Can you tell me where the stairs are?

The ladies disappear and I'm still in the stairwell. I take the garbage outside and practice yo-yoing. Shelesa comes down and we take turns. She's real good. When it gets dark we go back in. The elevator's still not working so we take the stairs.

THINGS I WON'T NEED TO REMEMBER ANYMORE

Sheri Simonsen

- My thirty-seven passwords

- Where I put the car keys

- Which foods to buy organic

- The name of that great new sushi place

- Is tomorrow garbage day?

TO HELL WITH CHICKEN LITTLE

Lasara Firefox Allen

My ten-year-old came home from school and asked, "Mom, is the world really going to end in twenty-twelve?"

Her question tossed me onto the jagged edge of my own internalized anger; this question was never supposed to happen. Not in my kid's mind.

I grew up with the constant and immanent threat that the sky was going to fall. I grew up in fear of the mushroom cloud, the Big One (the California Quake), the flu, whatever date was the next forecasted end-point. My dad used to half-joke about the day we'd have oceanfront property—after the rest of California had fallen into the sea.

I was raised as part of the Back-to-the-Land movement.

It was an experiment that had a lot going for it; living simply in an increasingly less-simple world is a thing of beauty; nights under a vast and starlit vault of sky. Living with and in the cycles of the seasons has an overwhelming grace to it. Learning to make due with what you have is a lesson we could all revisit. And homesteading brings localization to a fine point—forget the goal of sourcing your food from no further than fifty miles away, we're talking about under five acres.

But a cornerstone of the Back-to-the-Land movement was apocalyptic. The hippies who went to the hills weren't just running from "The Man," and not just "to the garden." They were running toward a safe zone—a place they'd be secure "when the shit comes down."

At once idealistic, fear-driven, naïve, and catastrophically reactionary, the Back-to-the-Land movement is perhaps best encapsulated by the juxtaposition of two ongoing projects from my youth:

In this corner, the garden—a literal garden, nearly as big as a city block, full of fresh and growing food, muddy feet, afternoon sweat, and an idyllic little shed that looks like a hobbit house. Eden in California.

And in the opposing corner, the bunker-sized bomb shelter dug into the side of the hill. Plans for filtration systems for air and water. Slow building stores of staple foods. Rations. And my questioning child-mind wondering why we would want to survive anything that would necessitate a bomb shelter.

Most 'Landers were devoted to the ideologies of post-capitalist, anti-authoritarian living. Many were highly educated free thinkers. And some were total wing-nuts, drawn to the edge because that's where they felt most comfortable. Some were all of the above. Most were also stuck in some level of fight or flight. Running from the draft, running from the law, running from the shirts and the talking heads, running from their own bad trips.

Even in the brightest of the "turned on, tuned in, and dropped out" avant-garde, there was a seething stickiness that seeped into the cracks between the culture that was "counter," and the culture it was countering against. Dark thoughts of the inevitable collapse. Infiltrators, Feds, counter-intelligence operatives, plants. Echoes of the Red Scare. Paranoia strikes deep.

In addition to the enshrined threat of natural and man-made disaster, there was a strong us/them mentality. "We"—the 'Landers—were "Us." Everyone else was "Them."

And "They" were out to get "Us."

This larger "They" wasn't the worker bees of the mainstream, but a nefarious entity that controlled the worker bees, too. "They" was The Man.

And so, as happens, a cornerstone of the belief-system I was born into formed a bedrock of fear and overwhelm. A bedrock that I rebel against to this day.

By the time the Y2K scare rolled around I had one kid and another on the way, we were living on the land where I grew up. Everyone we knew was stockpiling water, grains, seeds, fuel, candles, and more. The more radical stored up ammo for their rifles and shotguns.

It was a turning point for me. I made my decision to take a stand against the enculturation of fear. We didn't finish the bomb shelter my parents had started building when I was a kid. We didn't buy the 50 pound bag of rice. We didn't even get extra candles.

And you know what? The world didn't end. The System didn't crash. The grid didn't go down. Computers didn't glitch out and erase world economies.

Man, were there some bummed out hippies on 1/1/2000.

I felt vindicated, my intuition reinforced, my heart a little bit lighter for not having given in to the terror. I decided then and there I wouldn't raise my children to fear the world they live in.

Ten years later, here's my kid, looking me in the eye and asking for reassurance. And I tell her what I believe to be true: "No, honey. The world is not going to end in twenty-twelve."

Even though I know I can't control my kids' environments, anger surged toward my own faceless "Them." The "Them" that inculcates the next generation with a sense of doom.

I asked my daughter who had told her that the world would end, but the question was irrelevant; just like Y2K, just like during the cold war when we were all living "in the nuclear shadow," just like in the '80s with bird flu and the Harmonic Convergence, just like in 1500s when the plague was spreading like wildfire, just like 1000 CE when the Second Coming was certainly upon us, just like in any moment in any age… RIGHT NOW someone will lay out the facts as to the whys, hows, and wherefores of the absolutely incontrovertible FACT that The End is Nigh.

Most Back-to-the-Landers aren't even Christian, yet the simultaneously fear-driven and hope-inspired belief that, indeed, the shit WILL come down, mirrors the Christian apocalypse.

Some wait and pray for the downfall of "The Machine," imagining a day when the collapse of "The World As We Know It" will lead us through a magical doorway, and back into "the garden," a beautiful place where people will live in harmony with the land, sit around campfires, and build egalitarian communities.

Some believe that the only way to get to a new paradigm is to watch, or make, the old one burn.

Peak oil will happen. Maybe sooner, maybe later. But will we rise to the occasion and adapt to renewable energy sources?

The scientific proof that climate change is happening is absolute. But will science find ways for us to reverse the harm humanity has wrought on our global ecosystem?

War rages. Will that ever change?

Famine, climate change, war without end. Yes, these are truths. But signs that "The End" is at hand? I choose to think not.

I choose not to raise my children believing in doom.

I know I don't have the answers., only more questions.

What if we've been running in the wrong direction all this time?

What if there's a chance that there are positive effects of the globalization of culture? What if the shared global consciousness built by the Information Age is the step that will bring us together to create solutions that will create a new tomorrow that isn't based on a distinct end and a distinct beginning, but is instead founded in a gapping up of intelligence that comes from a connected, collective, conscious whole?

What if the internet and other avenues of cross-pollination hold a key to the next leap in our collective consciousness? What if currency were equalized, and resources were the basis of exchange? What if the simple act of teenagers who live in America, Israel, and Palestine creating friendships on social media sites leads a generation to learn how to build a world beyond boundaries?

Some may call me Pollyanna, or worse.

I'm well aware of the severity of our global predicament.

My secret dread is that maybe the shit IS actually coming down. Maybe we won't make the collective changes that need to be made in time. Maybe, even though it wasn't Y2K, or any of the other "This is it!" scares that have happened in my life and before it, maybe this IS it.

The core-reactor meltdown in Japan, the tidal wave, the earthquake, twisters in San Francisco, a hurricane in New York, evidence of climate change... my brain spins out, and I start losing sleep, and the nightmares start again. I'm still waiting for a revisit of the mushroom cloud, so ubiquitous in the dreamscape of my youth.

In my confusion, compounded by the exhaustion of a stress-induced lack of sleep—because I don't sleep when my dreams cease to be a refuge—the daily tensions mount. I get anxious. And teary. My stomach churns, my heart gets stuck in my chest, I can't breathe without really thinking about breathing, and when I have to think about breathing something is wrong.

I get scared. I question my own convictions, my sense of right and wrong. Maybe I'm being blasé. Maybe I should be hoarding matches, and canned food, and bottled water. Maybe I should have my kids take potassium iodide, or at least make them take kelp capsules.

And why don't we have a family emergency plan?

When the dread arises, the questions come.

Do I want to raise my children to love life or to fear death? Do I want to instill them with a fear response, conditioning their delicate fight/flight/freeze response to be set for perpetual red-alert? Or do I want to raise them knowing that regardless of what might happen next, right now they are safe?

Do I want to raise them to trust people, or to weave nihilistic, egoist tales of conspiracy? Do I want raise my children to believe in the nameless, faceless "Them"—a Hydra with innumerable heads and poisonous breath?

Or do I want to nurture my children into a gentle resilience, support them in growing their strong and beautiful core of humanitarian values and courageous action in support of unity and egalitarianism in the world as it already is? Do I want my children to naturally think beyond an "us" and a "them" into a place of "we?"

My answers are these; I choose to raise my children grounded strongly in a sense of justice and the possibility of effecting change. This is now, and now is what we make it. I choose not to frighten them with the specter of a post-apocalyptic tomorrow, nor do I promise them the return to some idealized garden, a mythical heaven on earth.

I choose to raise my children with their feet on the ground, and their hands reaching for the stars that glow in a future of their own making.

TRENDING

Sheri Simonsen

OUT	IN
Farmer's markets	Farming
Meat dresses	Meat
Sexting	Sextants
"Barefoot" shoes	Bare feet
iPads	Eye patches
Burning Man	Burning wood
Marijuana as medicine	Marijuana as currency

HAPPY ENDINGS

Kenna Lee

"You're going to dig that hole deeper before you put her in it, right?" the vet says, more order than question.

"Um, yes, of course. I was just, um, taking a break." The dog is beside me, beside the too-shallow hole I've dug, dead. All 100 pounds of her, thanks to the syringe the vet has now put away.

There's pretty much no graceful way to put a dead dog into a deep hole by yourself. She twists as she falls, forcing her neck backwards over her spine as she lodges in the dirt. I climb down in with her, dig out her head and unfurl the unnatural, painful pose. I curl her up to look comfy, then shovel the dirt back in, shovelful after shovelful, no matter that my back was already out before I started. This is what it means to be divorced. No one is going to bury the dog with you.

I spent my bygone marriage inching more and more toward my current belief that the world as we know it is ending, and it's up to us to figure out how to function in the new climate-changed one. I wasted one entire year out of the thirteen we were married suffocating in insomnia, tossing and turning under a blanket of anxiety about whether we should buy guns to protect ourselves and our garden from the possibility of violent foragers when the mainstream food supply chain broke down.

I obsessed about each and every decision, debating carbon footprints and sustainable methods, as if my stockpile of eco-righteous actions would form a talisman protecting my family against climate-related apocalypse. Turns out I should have been protecting my family from itself, or at least from the stranger who came to woo my wife away from neurotic, eco-obsessed, unsleeping me.

Three kids into the whole for-better-or-for-worse thing, she announced that she was moving on to greener pastures (or less green, if the frequent inclusion of disposable plastic containers in the kids' lunchboxes were any gauge). And I was worrying about the compost pile, about maximizing our food production, about learning the basics of seed-saving. Ka-boom. The sound of glass shards falling all around me. I always said that our Northern California community of lefty-liberal gardeners and tomato-canners was a bubble. I just never knew how brittle my own personal orb was. Crash. Tinkle.

Learning to say goodbye to your kids for three days every week feels about as good as having your face smashed into a piece of concrete into which the previously mentioned glass shards have embedded. And on top of the raw pain, the increased work hours necessitated by sudden sole responsibility for a mortgage, and the one-to-three parenting ratio during "my" days, not to mention the lethargy produced by post-separation depression, all conspire to make the allure of processed prepared foods and cheap non-organic burritos that someone else fixes and cleans up after more difficult than ever to resist. Before this divorce, my kids ate fresh local organic produce almost exclusively. But until the little white pills kick in, replacing my weeping lethargy with dry-eyed if Stepfordish functionality, the kids are eating frozen pizza, boxed mac &

cheese, and the kid-menu items at the cheap Mexican restaurant down the road. Finally (thank you, Lexapro), I get up from the couch and start to seek out—what is it those annoyingly optimistic get-off-the-couch books call it? Ah, yes: The opportunity in the crisis.

And since I have no other choice, really, I find it. In the dreary aftermath of the implosion of my nuclear family, I am dragged kicking and whining into redefining my values, looking at my choices, and owning up to my responsibilities on this new, revised planet as never before. And despite myself and my self-pity, the larger picture of how I want to create my own community, my own sustainability, and of course, my permaculture garden, comes slowly more and more into focus. I want to teach my children skills I barely have: How to grow a garden without the nursery that sells us the plants, how to hatch and slaughter chickens, how to live with more community than commerce.

And this is what it means to be divorced. No one is going to slaughter the chickens with you, but neither are they going to stand in your way. It turns out I'm not really lonely as I plant my fruit trees one by one, a foot-high spindly pomegranate replacing a dying decorative bush, a slow removal of invasive stalky weeds to make room for the orange tree I'll buy myself for my birthday this year. Where the dog is buried, she will decompose and feed our slowly expanding blueberry patch as it inches down the hill.

That almost sounds like a happy ending. I want that happy ending so much, I keep writing it over and over. Still, there's no guarantee. Maybe the blueberries will all fall off in a drought, maybe the tomato plants will shrivel up again this year. Maybe half the chickens will die from intestinal parasites the week before we plan to butcher them, and we'll toss the carcasses in the trash bin to go to unsustainable, methane-producing landfill, afraid of keeping the bodies around. Not every animal around here gets a decent burial. There was the pony, poor old Freckles, hauled away without dignity by the knacker.

Freckles was never very fast, but he began slowing down significantly by the time Child Number 3 was old enough to sit on him. He limped more and more, we rode less and less, and I dispensed his painkillers liberally. The day he didn't bother to come up for his food, I called the vet. I explained to the kids that Freckles was hurting, and that the vet was coming, and if she couldn't make him feel better, then she would help him die so he wouldn't have to be in pain.

"Can we cut Freckles' tail off?" Number 2 immediately asked.

"Um, no," I stammered, tripped up by this unexpected request. It seemed almost obscene, callous. "Freckles might want his tail to swat away the flies while we wait for the vet to come."

"Well, if he dies, can we cut it off?"

"Um, well, let me think about that," I deferred. We went on about our morning, bringing Freckles his last meal out to where he was standing unmoving, having our own breakfast. It seemed like a normal day.

"Mom," Child Number 2 piped up an hour or so later. "If Freckles dies, can we cut off his feet?"

"Um, uh, his feet?"

"Yeah. We could make bowls out of them and use them and always remember him."

"Um, well, I think it would be really messy to cut off his feet, so I don't think I want to do that."

"Oh. Okay." Time for Legos, off he went.

Later in the morning, we went down to check on the pony. Number 2 regarded him with a thoughtful tilt of his head. "Mom, can we eat Freckles?"

At this point, he had pretty much rendered me speechless, but I made an effortful recovery. "If we were really hungry, and didn't have enough food to eat or money to buy more, then we would probably eat Freckles. But we have plenty of food, and Freckles wouldn't taste very good, so we are not going to eat him." I willed him not to ask what was going to happen to the body once the knacker man came to haul him away, and he didn't. So we just waited for the vet to arrive, and I tried to reconcile my sweet son's loving heart with the fact that he so pragmatically suggested first dismembering, and then eating, our pet.

And then I got it. My son is not a budding psychopath, but rather a total ecologist. He was just verbalizing the values I'd been trying, in my half-assed way, to teach him: Reduce, reuse, recycle. It's not that he didn't care about ornery Freckles, it's just that he was able to envision a continued usefulness for him beyond the traditional pony-rides. He was way ahead of me.

Inspired, I tried to figure out how to honor this vision without crossing my personal boundary of "too yucky." Presumably the knacker man would be using Freckles' leftovers in some way, though I was pretty sure I didn't want to ask how. I briefly considered renting a backhoe and burying him myself so we could have a family discussion about how Freckles was nourishing our land, but I wasn't sure of the legality of burying livestock in my neighborhood. By the time the vet was able to make it over, the boys had gone off for a long-planned playdate, so Number 2 missed seeing Freckles slump slowly to the ground and grow still. And he also missed the vet's unexpected question after she ascertained that there was no heartbeat: "Do you want me to cut off his tail?"

Clearly outvoted, I acquiesced, dividing the tail into two long elastic-bound literal ponytails for the boys to do with what they would—whip each other, apparently, then decorate their room. Eventually they ended up back outside, forgotten, and for a few seasons now, all the bird's nests I find are threaded through with long white hairs.

Is that a happy ending? With the icecaps still melting? I think not. But there's consolation in the nest-entangled white hairs. There's beauty in the sweet peas I grow from last year's saved seeds, in the smooth brown egg my daughter pulls out warm from under a noisy chicken. There's blind hope in the crazy forest of avocado trees popping up around my compost pile. It's all incredibly fragile, these worlds we build. The sound of glass shards falling all around us. The remote possibility that we will tenaciously, miraculously survive.

five **CATACLYSMS**

I think this is irresponsible preaching and very dangerous, and especially when it is slanted toward children, I think it's totally irresponsible, because I see nothing biblical that points up to our being in the last days, and I just think it's an outrageous thing to do, and a lot of people are making a living—they've been making a living for 2,000 years—preaching that we're in the last days.

—CHARLES M. SCHULZ

THE RUSSIANS

Kitty Torres

"Alright class," Sister Helen, the tiny ancient nun said. "Please stand up by the side of your desks."

It's October of 1962 and I am a Third Grader at St. Augustine's Grammar School. The children all look at each other, confused. Get up in the middle of a history lesson?

"Now the Principal will be making an announcement and I want everyone to get under their desks after the announcement."

Regina McBride sits directly across from me. Her lip quivers like she's about to cry.

The P.A. cracks on, continues to crack and sizzle during the announcement.

"Attention boys and girls, this is your Principal speaking. We are going to conduct a drill to see how fast you can lie underneath your desks. On the count of three, please get up from your seat and lie face down on the floor under your desk. One…. Two… Three."

Like all twenty-eight of my classmates, I do as I'm told and I lay on the floor, I tilt my head to the right and see Regina McBride, still holding back tears and shaking.

"Don't cry," I whisper.

Regina nods and turns her head the other way.

Sister Helen's face appears next to mine. She has two enormous white whiskers on her chin that match the white of her habit.

"Silence, please!" She hisses.

"Sorry, Sister." I mumble. Now I want to cry, too.

The minute feels like forever before the Principal comes back on the P.A.: "Children, please get up and sit back at your desks. The drill is now over."

"What do you think it means?" I ask Regina when we're out on the lunch yard.

"What?"

"This morning getting under our desks?"

"My father said something very serious is going on, and I should pray for peace... every night."

James Martin runs by yelling, "The Russians are behind it all, you'll see." He grabs his orange basketball out of a bush and sprints out of the girls' area.

"The Russians," Regina spits. "I hate those communists."

At home in her room, Mom talks on our black telephone, her Benson & Hedges extra long cigarette clamped in her teeth. She hums, "Mmmmmmm, and Hhhhhhhmmmmmm" as she folds cloth diapers. She takes the cigarette out of her mouth and stabs it several times in the Waterford crystal ashtray as blue smoke meanders through the air.

"Listen," she says into the phone. "Kathy just came in and I have to go. Yes, I'll call soon. God bless." She hangs up. "How was school?"

"Fine."

"Can you help me fold these diapers? I want to start dinner."

"O.K. but before you go, I want ask you something."

"Sure, what is it?"

"Do you know why we had to hide under our desks at school today? Are the Russians going to invade us?"

"Who told you that?" She gets up and grabs her ashtray, walking toward the door.

"James Martin said it was on account of the Russians."

"That James is too smart."

"Are the Russians going to attack us, Mom?"

"Mother, please call me Mother."

"What does it mean, Mother?"

"This is nothing a little girl should have to worry about, it's nothing really."

I fold the diapers, then and set the table. Mother wants me to watch Gregg and Mary while she makes a phone call—door shut. She carries her ashtray, matches and B&H box with her. That means it will be a long call.

Gregg plays on the floor, making towers with his blocks and knocking them over. Mary watches, fascinated, trying to reach the blocks through the bars of her play pen. Gregg has learned to build them just far enough away.

I look out the front window and hope Dad will be home soon. Maybe he'll tell me what's going on.

But when Dad gets home, Greg cries "Dad—deeee!" and runs and grabs his leg.

"Not now, son. Let me hang up my coat."

Gregg frowns.

Mary holds her hand out of the playpen. "Dadadadada!"

Finally, after dinner, after the newscasters have informed him that the Cuban Missile Crisis continues, and she's playing peek-a-boo with Mary and I have my chance: "Dad, they made us hide under our desks today."

"Oh?" He gives Mary one more peek.

"A boy in my class says the Russians are behind it. What do you think?"

"Did you ask your mother about this?"

I start to walk away; my parents will bounce me like a tennis ball between them. I nod, head into to my room to finish reading the book that I have to write a report on.

As I close the door I hear my mother whisper, "Let's pray they never have to get under those desks again."

THE PLANES

Kate Dreyfus

The second plane is crashing into the building. It's tilted sideways. The left wing is down the right wing up. As it enters the building, black smoke billows. Maybe it's not so bad, maybe not so bad as it looks, and anyhow I'm on a conference call. I'm on a lawyer conference call. I'm working at home and I've got the television on, volume turned down to whispers, because just before the conference call a friend called and said "Turn on your television." I did, but then I turned it down for the call.

On the phone we're arguing pleasantly about which insurer owes who a duty to clean up the toxic chemicals under this particular bridge in this particular city. One after another the lawyers are performing solos of righteous indignation. In between my talking parts I mute the phone and turn the TV back on, then mute the TV and turn the phone back on. It'll be some time before we learn that Janna's husband died in there, trapped above an embedded plane, no way out—was he the falling man?

The buildings are burning both the towers are burning I am thinking oh it's not so bad, really, they look just fine below the point of impact, I think this is going to be just fine, and the lawyer for insurer of the southernmost property owner is pointing out the key exclusions in the policy language, and noting that there is no coverage here, truly there is no coverage, or in the alternative, if there were coverage, it was negated by the actions of the insured, the bad acts of the insured, and then someone asks if we have heard, have we heard about the Towers? Yes we have, we have all heard, and now we return to the issue at hand, the issue of coverage, and do all the participants on the line have the coverage timeline that Frank prepared? Yes we do. The coverage periods all laid out in sideways rectangles, across the page, like sideways towers.

The call begins to collapse in on itself. We end it in a round of self-congratulation on our progress. We schedule a follow-up for the same time next week.

I go out the back door to the garden. I like my garden. It's pleasant and peaceful and calm. My daughter thinks it's messy. She has many suggestions for improvements. But she's more interested in announcements than action.

This garden, or yard, whatever you want to call it, is particularly challenged in September. That's when the figs turn gold and fall to explode on the brittle-straw grass.

I don't water the grass. Not out of any principled position, it's more a matter of time, and economy of time. Watering takes time. Water goes only where it is essential: Tomatoes, beans, the eighteen blueberry bushes.

Sometimes when I sit here alone, after the transfer of my child to her other house, the dog comes out and joins me. He likes to bask in the sun and heat, four white legs splayed out, joints swiveled outwards. The cat hides her grey and white body in the cool of the green hedge, watchful, eyes dilated, blue and vacant skies. But today, it's just me.

I like my garden in September. My yard—whatever you want to call it.

The leaves of the edamame beans are yellow but I leave them there, remembrance of the beans. The tomatoes go sideways in search of more space and crawl their way out of their assigned places. And the pole beans, twirled like ringlets of hair around their poles, still blossoming, still sending out beans for me to watch and water.

Cantor Fitzgerald. That's where Janna's husband works.

Also in the garden, I have my apple tree, and my pear. They are good to me, year after year. Forgiving, asking nothing, they send out fruit.

I am far away, in Portland. Port and land. Serene and green. 3000 miles away. Surely no one is aiming a plane at us?

The sky is too blue. The air too quiet. Restless, I go back inside to stand before the whispering television. The first tower has fallen. It fell just like that in a poof of smoke like a poof of a mushroom puff ball it's gone.

I cannot reach my mother. The lines are all jammed. Which way is the smoke blowing? Is it toxic smoke? My mother is less than a mile north of the towers, by the river. Is she O.K.? Is she watching television? Or is she oblivious, sitting in the den, listening to classical music, humming and reading The New York Times?

In the kitchen, I turn the tap on and let the water run. After all, there's lead in the pipes. It's best to let the water run for a minute, that's what the utility company says. I pour myself a glass of water, and take it outside to the garden. I look to the sky, and wait, for the sound of planes.

THE MOTORCYCLE GANG'S JACKET

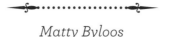

Matty Byloos

The Motorcycle Gang wore brown, believing it to be the synthesis of all colors, and therefore, all things. The crest on the back of the brown leather jacket told the whole story of The Motorcycle Gang's mission, and of everything that was to come in the remaining days before the end.

In the center, a house made of red-brown bricks and black bricks and other bricks that were yellow – the color of sand. And anyone looking could see inside this house – it was torn open for all, baring its truth the way a shark opens its mouth underwater, telling a story.

A Siamese bear sat at a table, four long knives in each of its fours hands and two wolverine skins sewn together into a bathrobe over both of its heads. The bear's genitalia, highly articulated in the image, was human, and could be seen underneath the table. That flesh was more fleshed out than any other flesh depicted on that jacket.

Three white tigers slept quietly at the bear's feet on a white cloud that had been flattened into a rug. A silver scale hung by a golden chain from the bottom of the house, which floated in the brown leather sea that was The Motorcycle Gang's back. Dead animals surrounded the floating house on both sides, their dark crimson pools of blood depicted in precious stones.

A church organ hung in the air to the left, became a silent movie theater in its severity, all its black and white keys exposed and useless, a fallen zebra coiled into a crescent shape at its pedals.

A blank-covered book tilted to a three-quarter profile occupied the air to the right of the house, a polished black leather cover and the crisp bone white of its pages exposed. A panda bear sliced almost in two slipped out from its middle.

A sea of cartoon men's faces, each containing no more than a single eye and a black hole for a mouth, peered out from behind every side of the house. Rainbow pyramids of light shot out from every toothless hole and a lunar eclipse rose up toward The Motorcycle Gang's neck. A pattern of densely clustered triangles lined the bottom of the image near the waist, a jagged sea of black, white and red.

EROTALYPTICA

Bonnie Ditlevsen

A magnet on my refrigerator says *Please don't tell me to relax—it's my tension that's holding me together.*

I sent Connor and Kylie out to the swingset, even though it's a Bad Air Day. Third one this week, and we're only at Thursday. Pretty soon they'll be calling them Bad Air Weeks.

And I'm eating carrots. So sue me.

What I'm hearing on the radio—my little ball radio from back in the day, good thing I saved it all these years, because radios are now in BIG demand—is that the World Wide Web is permanently down, and won't be up anytime soon, as in my lifetime. Same as what they said about cable television a month ago. It's all from the Mars asteroids, the new diocryocin contamination.

You might think me a bad mother for sending the kids out to play, but the way I see it, there's no research yet to prove that a little exposure to diocryocin won't hurt, won't build up tolerance. Resistance. Kind of like how my mother used to let me get good and dirty as a kid. Everyone needs to eat a little dirt, Sarah, she told me. Otherwise you just get sick all the time.

How odd, really, that the word diocryocin has the letters c-r-y in it. Crying is all I've been doing these days, though I don't let the kids or Jeffrey see me. I've only cried in my room, with the door shut. I used to cry there in the past about how I'd never use my anthropology degree, not while raising two kids. But what hurt the most was that I was halfway through floral design school when I got pregnant. I'd make an excellent florist if only the planets in this solar system would cooperate more.

Of all the careers on earth, Jeffrey had to go to work for FEMA—emergency disaster management. Homeland Security is what it really is. And now he's gone more than he's here. Satellites failing, cable communications and phones down, and whoops! There goes my husband for another three weeks. I rely on the radio broadcasts, which are frequent. We have batteries still. A lot of people's radios are the plug-in kind, so when the rolling blackouts are in effect, I sometimes get neighbors knocking for news updates.

***

Adolph Hitler, Josef Stalin, atomic bomb, Pol Pot, napalm, Spanish-conquistador smallpox, you've all got nothing on diocryocin. Whatever human beings thought up throughout history to off one another is chump change compared to what the planet Mars had in store for us here on earth. And when I mention the diseases the Spaniards brought to the Americas in the 15th and 16th centuries, I can only shake my head: The Mayans they met up with were right all along. We're goners now.

The Valentine's Asteroids were what kicked it off, the actual event spanning the 13th through 16th of February. Looking back, I have to laugh. The news morons and the pundits all bitched about retail sales for that weekend, how restaurants and stores lost all their business because people stayed indoors or hid in their basements. Everything was prefaced by, "In this economy, blah blah blah…," when the fact of the matter was, Earth was being peppered with that diocryocin shit, and no one realized it. So while they were busy worrying about consumer indices and quarterly earnings, the rest of us were looking out our windows and wondering about the fine dust everywhere. It looked like those old photos of Mount St. Helens back in the 1980s, volcanic ash everywhere.

But here's the crazy part: Our water tested completely fine. While NASA and the scientists all tried to determine the origins of the dust, and its chemical composition, several winter weather systems coated us with snow and ice, and pretty soon it became clear that the dust would soak into the earth and get into streams, rivers, the water table, and so on, eventually becoming our tap water. Lo and behold, the lab tests showed that the asteroid dust didn't bond with H_2O. Ever wonder why Mars has no water? Your answer is: diocryocin. Think oil and vinegar, and you'll get the idea.

Despite the asteroid crashes that Valentine's weekend, some of which crushed cars and houses in Iowa, Poland and some country ending in -stan, and despite the film of dust everywhere that raised the big alarm, we could all go to the sink and get ourselves a nice tall glass of water. When you can do that, it's amazing how normal you feel after disaster strikes.

So by March, people relaxed. It was officially revealed that we'd been pummeled by billions of teeny-tiny pieces of the polar areas of Mars—and no one had an explanation as to why.

Well, I think the Mayans knew why. I think they're laughing at us from their graves, hunch-kneed skeletons wrapped in gauze, cackling from their little round burial pits. They knew way back then about this. They knew.

Starbucks and Cinnabon opened back up, and all was well.

Men bought their wives shiny thong underwear and Very Sexy Push-Up bras at Victoria's Secret. Made up for the February 14th disaster and whatnot.

But when winter ended and spring began, the farmers, and then biologists, and then the media began to report the effects of diocryocin on plant roots. Ever touch a fern, only to see it recoiling? Ever blanch fresh spinach in a pan? That's what was going on underground, in the soil. Countless billions of plant roots, big and small, gasping their last breaths, weakening and then withering, and then from the roots up, dying.

That was late May, the Global Browning. A few spots on the planet were spared: deserts, of course. And one valley in western Australia, curiously enough. Panicked people with money began flying to Perth in droves, trying to buy land. The rest of us just checked our refrigerators and pantries: noodles, rice, dried beans, cans of Dinty Moore. It was a horror, especially since from every car window on every highway, the devastation of plants and the browning of tree leaves could be seen at a time of year when everything was supposed to be all shades of green.

But we had our 9 to 5 jobs, our convenience stores, our graceful subdivisions, our comfy lives. No one imagined that the diocryocin problem would last beyond a couple of good rainy weekends. Things would green right up again.

Knowing that our water was safe, we bought that last fresh produce from California and Florida and the Carolinas. We smoked diocryocin-laced tobacco, ate bean sprouts and bag lettuce with diocryocin in its veins, and munched on cucumbers and carrots without thinking.

The side effects at first were curious: tingling in one's genital area, slight shortness of breath, and lightheadedness. Counties advised people to eat canned or dried food, and to limit fresh products. Some heeded the warning, some didn't. I found I was giddy in the kitchen, making the kids some Ramen or some boxed Rice a Roni, all the while nibbling at chopped lettuce.

I looked at my boss at the temp agency as a conquest now, even though he was a blubbery, ugly married man with grown kids who never called or visited him.

I pestered Jeffrey all the time for sex, all night, and though he liked the attention at first, he began to wonder about it.

"With so much going on out there," he said one night in the dark of our bedroom, as I straddled his hips, wishing his cock hadn't given out, "do you think your horniness might be chemical?"

"Chemical? I feel great. What do you mean?"

"Well, you weren't ever like this before."

"I was! In college, I was."

"Um, I was with you all though college, Sarah. You weren't…like this." And he took his hand around the small of my back, and rolled me off of him, which was his signal to lay off. To get some sleep.

His FEMA job had become more of one in which he spent all day placating angry farmers and related suppliers, shipping companies and the like, all of whom were losing revenue.

By early June, the tingling was so great that I was sucking off my boss and getting quickies at the Subaru dealership for minor things such as an oil change. I was meeting up with Kylie's friend Emily's father, another person still eating fresh veg. I was even hooking up with people on Facebook, guys I'd only vaguely known from my huge high school class. Without Emily's dad and the regular thing with my boss, I'd have exploded, I think. Diocryocin is an itch. An itch you just have to scratch.

And I wasn't the only one. Pretty soon, you could tell who kept eating the remaining fresh produce the stores were selling, and who wasn't. The "grainers"—people avoiding diocryocin-laced foods—were the ones NOT screwing around like rabbits, and those of us who were, well, we were a community. When Emily's mom moved out of their house, leaving behind the words FUCKING PIG purple spray painted in all caps on the door of her two-car garage, we got the terrific idea to ship Emily over to my house, so as to host sex parties at Emily's dad's. We throw a large sheepskin rug over the huge green billiard table in his finished basement. It's become my throne.

"Mommy," Connor told me one evening, as I dolled up to go out, "I don't think it's safe to leave us kids here all alone. I get scared."

"Nooo, sweetheart," I cooed. "You're fine. There's the three of you! I popped you some Orville Redenbacher. Watch TV and just pretend it's a sleepover."

"Well, it IS a sleepover!" Kylie protested. "You never come home from Emily's until the next day!"

"Mommy's itchy," I said, now serious. "And so is Emily's daddy. That's why I go there. Now go watch Invader Zim and I'll see you in the morning."

Back when 9/11 happened, I was so young. Twenty-six, just a couple of years out of college. I remember how I watched the footage over and over until I couldn't take it anymore. I went to the sunroom of the crappy apartment Jeffrey and I were renting in Toledo, and I sat down by the spider plants and little jade trees, looking at their shiny leaves, thinking, Why? Why?

After that, life returned to normal, save for a few big changes, like the notion of terrorism as a part of everyday fears, and those color-coded levels of threat posted in airports, at police departments, announced on the nightly news, and so on.

For eleven years, life went on as it should. Jeffrey and I had the kids. We bought this house.

We worked on our marriage.

***

We're living out a slow September 11th now.

It's August, and I've screwed about as much of Lucas, Wood, Monroe, and Sandusky Counties as I can. The scientific evidence of diocryocin's effect on the nervous system—irreversible effects, I might add—came to light in July. All around the world, especially countries with less processed food and more farm-to-table traditions, citizens were abandoning their moral codes, screwing like wildfire. Even in some Middle Eastern countries where an adulterer would normally be stoned to death, there were few who could, or would, cast the first stone.

A frenzy.

Before the Internet went down, and before it became clear that the Mars toxins were more numerous and complex than just diocryocin and thelanate xiamerol, I heard a report that online searches and sales of the Kama Sutra were unprecedented, and that stores couldn't even begin to keep up with the print demand.

"I won't eat those vegetables you've frozen," Jeffrey said on one of the last visits here. He picked at his plate of fettuccine, disgusted. "I'm trying to save this planet. That's my job. I see you have a very different agenda now, Sarah."

We've got flooding now, and areas like mine that haven't been flooded out are seeing more displaced people. I've had several come knocking at my door, and some just sleep out on my deck without my permission. Emily's dad and I have used this to our advantage for the orgy parties. We lock up our stockpile of dry food to make sure we aren't taken advantage of when our fuckfests happen. We also take in our rain barrels, since the water company has gone bust, and service is now so random.

Sometimes, some of the people at our parties are in fact ones who were careful in the beginning not to eat fresh produce. They're ones who come, and writhe and pretend they want to be a part of it all, but you can sense that they're just hungry, and hoping we'll feed them once we've orgied with them. I have to tell Connor and the kids to guard the house at night, because there might be some crazy person breaking in, just to scrounge around for something to eat.

The radio says that there are reports of animals dying en masse in Central America, and that the biosphere will be permanently altered by this. Fires are raging in areas that used to be rainforest.

As for me, like so many others, I have sex on my mind. A good fucking. Money won't be much good any longer, now that stores are being looted and gas stations are out of fuel. I heard they're fighting at the refineries.

I heard that a Mars probe back in 2011 might have triggered all of this. Some series of explosions NASA set off, some test for precious minerals there. Something about a robotic vehicle malfunctioning, sending a premature signal for them to go ahead and detonate.

I am a Mayan fertility goddess, naked in Emily's dad's basement with my mouth around someone' huge cock, someone else's fingers ramming me, and another guy's hands grabbing and twisting my breasts like dials.

THE END TIMES PROJECT

Yasmin Elbaradie

We practiced in advance. The siren went off once a month and we'd all go under our desks, like that would protect us. We must have looked like animals at the zoo, the thin bars of the desk legs and the chair's wooden tops forming our cages. Of course, it wasn't the end of the world we were practicing for—just the end as we knew it, if Iraq decided to re-invade Kuwait.

One time we tried to play a prank on our Arabic teacher in the second grade. He hadn't arrived to the classroom yet and we decided to seize this golden opportunity.

"Quick, get under the desks," Shiva, called out. She was Iranian with a long ponytail.

We scrambled to comply, giggling from under our desks. Ostaz Hamada walked in. He was tall and thin, with a black moustache above his lips.

"You think you're birds? Too small to be seen hiding under your desks?" He suppressed laughter. He grabbed the chalkboard eraser to wipe off the previous lesson. "Schadenfreude: mirth at someone else's misfortune," I read before it was gone.

The practicing didn't help much.

It was June, and Suzy and I were in our raft, paddling down the Nile. She was doing a last-minute check over supplies.

"Did you get the whistle?"

"Whistle? What do we need that for?"

"I told you. It was on the list—on the Facebook group. Egyptians for Emergency Preparedness Efforts."

"Shit."

"You use it to signal for help or scare predators away," she sighed. "Tell me you got the protein powder at least."

I pulled out the large, plastic container from my backpack, relieved.

She grabbed it and inspected it. "This has soy in it! I told you to get the on hundred percent hemp kind. So no whistle and GMOs in our protein source. I'm not sure if we should even bother following the rest of the embankment plan."

I was trying to formulate a response when a bolt of lightening shot through the sky. I looked up, and there was Neptune, the god, holding his pitchfork and wearing his luminous crown, long gray hair and beard flowing just like in my Usborne Greek Mythology Illustrated book. He looked a little like an aging hippy, but angrier and more muscular. What was the God of the Sea doing in the sky?

Suzy shook her head. "It's O.K., we'll manage without the protein powder.

Neptune seemed to be looking right at me. He grabbed his pitchfork and waved it and another lightening bolt erupted, fragmenting across the dusky sky. Bats and birds squawked and flew in confused circles.

I thought I heard him shout, "It's not for you mortals to determine the place of the gods."

Suzy startled and jerked back. "Quick, paddle."

"We can't get away from him."

"We can try."

I obeyed, the adrenaline kicking in so my arms weren't sore until later.

Suzy prodded me with her oar. "Are you planning to sleep the whole trip?"

"Sorry." I hadn't realized I'd fallen asleep.

We were no longer in Cairo. The river had grown wider, and there was an absence of buildings on either side of the shore. Nubian boys in little half boats surrounded us. They used their hands as paddles, and shouted, "Hello, welcome Egypt!"

On the riverbank there were all kinds of animals—polar bears, elephants, deer. We saw Boogey and Tumtum, the monsters that had been beneath the Great Wall of China. They were obese and fleshy, like Sumo wrestlers. My skin crawled as I watched them consume animals whole. I was grateful they were too busy eating to notice our boat.

"I've been thinking," Suzy began, letting her oar glide over the water's surface for a second. "I know I said you could tag along on my escape plan, but I think I want to change it."

I stopped rowing.

"I need to be alone." Suzy rowed to shore, jumped out, and dragged the boat onto the bank. I hadn't realized she meant her revised plan would be effective immediately. She pointed up at a hill. "There's a monastery up there. I'm going to go talk to the monk."

She turned to me, an afterthought: "I know you're an atheist, but you're welcome to spend a few days up here, before you figure out what you'll do." She smiled kindly at me, the way you would to a mother struggling to push up a double-wide stroller uphill, then reached into her cargo short pockets to hand me a few gold coins. "Good luck."

I wanted to follow her because I had no idea what else to do, but a sense of pride stopped me. I could figure this out on my own. I didn't need her. Especially with the way she'd been treating me.

I sat down, let my feet get wet as the water lapped at the shore. I was happy I had my hat. It was evidence that I wasn't as undependable as she thought. But I didn't have my lip balm, and licked my lips, anxious.

My parents had gone to Thailand. It was the one place my father could stand, and my mom had decided she wanted to accompany him. My sister was at the Libyan border with the refugees.

My brother had built an underground bunker in his backyard in the suburbs. His plan was well thought-out, and precisely designed to accommodate one person. "The oxygen supply, the food store, everything," he explained. "Having another person would defeat the whole purpose; there wouldn't be any point in being down there." He spoke to me like I was a simpleton, and I suspected he'd designed it for one person on purpose, subscribing to Sartre's philosophy that hell was other people.

My ex had barely changed his life. Work, videogames. He told me he was eating ice cream everyday.

It seemed everyone had a plan for living out the end of the world except me.

It had all been precisely calculated. Sun Myung Moon had spent a billion dollars on securing the world's best religion experts. It took three years and was known as the End Times Project. They pored over the world's religious texts—not only the major religions but all kinds of tiny and obscure faiths—and decided, once and for all, when the world would end.

I remember watching Sun Myung on CNN. "It's ridiculous… to be living in such an advanced society, and still not know when the end of the world is," he'd said. "Thanks to my stockholders, in a matter of years we will know exactly."

The liberals mocked him at the beginning. I wasn't sure. It seemed far off, but the world was a mysterious place.

The End Times Project was publicly traded, and when the date was announced, the stock price quadrupled overnight. People were worried there'd be a bubble.

Some people referred to it as a prediction at first. Except it wasn't; it was fact. 2027.

The obvious things happened initially—people flocked to churches, mosques, and temples. But it was still a long way off. People couldn't attend church for a decade.

I woke up to loud squawks and jet-black ravens circling. If my mother were there she would've said it: Bad sign.

My stomach growled and I remembered the energy bar in my pocket. It was gummy and tasted fake-sweet, but it was better than hunger.

I walked along the water's edge. The only time I'd been up here was for a Nile cruise, years ago, with the rest of my family. I was a teenager then. The world was in a bad place, but only the most hardcore environmentalists thought we were screwed. Greenpeace ranted about the rainforest's decimation and the ozone hole grew like a run in stockings. Cairo had always looked like it was on the brink of apocalypse, with the dubious honor of being the world's most polluted city several years running.

"Hoda!" someone yelled.

At the water's edge a pale woman washed her Godiva-long hair.

I startled. "Do I know you?"

She took me in for a hug. Whispered in my ear, "I'm Aphrodite."

I shivered. Her face was that of an older woman, but she was still beautiful.

When she let me go, we were surrounded by dogs. They were tall and lean; maybe greyhounds. One licked Aphrodite's feet and she giggled.

She urged me to change out of my khakis and button-down shirt and into a summery dress which did wonders for my cleavage. She took my hair out of its ponytail and pinned it on top of my head. Finally she applied expensive make-up to my face. I went along willingly.

We spent the day picking berries. I forgot about the end times. I never wanted to leave Aphrodite's side. A utopian apocalypse.

She introduced me to each of her dogs, and I liked them as much as I liked her.

As the sun set, a dining table appeared out of nowhere with a spread far too large for the two of us. I ate and ate, and she pulled out a strawberry pie at the end, still warm.

After dinner, Aphrodite produced a backgammon board and we played for hours. When I began to yawn, in full expectation that Aphrodite would offer me a place to rest my head, that night and for all nights, she snapped her fingers in front of my face.

"You cannot stay."

I thought she was joking. "But...why not?"

"There are rules. You have had a full day of nurturing. More than that and you will grow soft and lazy and believe yourself above your station."

Her words were a shock of cold water.

She stroked my cheek with her fingertips. Coming from anyone else, it would've angered me. Instead I rose, thinking: This is my fate.

I spent the night cross-legged, staring at the river.

The first thing I saw when I opened my eyes was a man I didn't know, sitting next to me and obviously waiting for something.

"Good morning," he said.

I rose to sitting. "Who are you?"

"I was wondering if you wanted a job."

I blinked back sleep. "A job? I can't afford a job."

"This is the old kind of job. The kind that pays."

A job that paid was either dirty or dangerous.

"Don't worry, it's not too bad," he said, reading my mind.

He wore shorts and no top, and one of his ears had a small hoop through it. He walked with a limp, but it didn't slow him down.

"I'm Adel," he said as I followed him.

"Hoda."

A few years ago people started quitting their jobs in waves. The New York Times called it the "The New Economy." People figured they would live off their savings until the end times rolled around. With a lack of workers, production of most traditional goods slowed to a crawl. Capitalists weren't exactly motivated either– why invest when it's all going to end? But the workaholics still needed to work, so they paid to work. Monthly dues, like a gym membership.

Of course, poor people couldn't afford to coast for a few years. They had no savings. And there were still things people wanted—Xboxes, iPhones, garbage service. Those jobs were still out there. The ones no one had ever wanted.

I wasn't exactly rich or poor. With my own limited funds, I'd been scraping by.

We walked away from the Nile and into the desert. I panicked a little—he was a strange man, after all—but Adel seemed laid-back.

We arrived at a construction site where lots of workers were milling around. The sun seared our flesh; I heard the loud buzzing of a fly, and in the distance, the clanking of metal on metal. A boxy one-story building had the word Allah spray-painted on it in Arabic.

I followed Adel because I couldn't stand the idea of being by myself, obsessing about the horror stories Mrs. Safwan had described in eleventh grade religion class about the end of the world, when mothers wouldn't recognize their children from the terror. I knew I wouldn't survive on my own, mentally or physically. I felt like a crushing failure—everyone else had a plan, but there was no room in anyone's plan for me.

"Are you paying attention?" Adel asked, and then I was. He explained what I'd have to do. "First you put on this bodysuit—it's not exactly DKNY—then you go in this little tube, like an MRI. It's freaky the first time, but you get used to it fast. It shoots you up—"

"I'm not paying you to chat," someone yelled.

"I'm showing the new girl the ropes." Adel turned to face me. "You'll figure it out."

I climbed into the bodysuit, which was white and heavy and smelled of someone else's sweat.

It was lucky to find a real job, I thought. And it didn't sound too bad. It'd be a good way to kill time before—well, you know.

The job was simple. They'd shoot you up in the pod, and you had something that looked like a rake, and you would scrape the clouds. There were plastic bags suspended beneath them to capture the rain droplets that formed from raking the clouds. I found it meditative. This clean water would be bottled and shipped to the rich people who could afford to drink it. I'd gotten used to the dirty water, like most everyone else. At least we had water.

Adel handed me a business card. "Now here's a real vintage item. We still have these left over, so you might as well have one."

I studied the small rectangle. The card was silvery and made of thick cardstock. The embossed text read Cloud Harvester. Below, in a smaller font, The Dream Corporation. And all the way at the bottom, in font so small you needed to squint: A subsidiary of MonsantoSunMoonTimeWarner, Inc.

I found that the job fit me like an old glove. It gave me something to do, and shelter, food, a sense of safety. I liked Adel. He was friendly, and seemed relaxed about the end of the world. At night we stayed up watching old episodes of Jay Leno on his laptop.

But one day while I was up raking, I was consumed with a sudden urge to taste the water. When I thought no one was looking, I dipped my finger into the water in one of the plastic bags and stuck it in my mouth. It was cold and tasted like nothing, like I remembered. I thought of the Dream Corporation billboards that had been plastered all over Cairo. So that's what clean and pure tasted like.

"Should've warned you about that," was the first thing Adel told me when I climbed out of the landing pod.

"What?"

"Employee 21470," a loudspeaker boomer.

"That's you," Adel said. "Sorry."

They'd seen me.

I walked into a small, upscale office. The man behind the desk had platinum hair and icy blue eyes.

"Welcome." He clasped his hands on his desk and smiled. "I take it you were not aware of the presence of the video cameras monitoring you as you harvested the clouds."

I shook my head. He reached for a remote from somewhere beneath his desk and pressed a button. A small TV in the corner lit up and I saw a video of myself tasting the water.

"Do you understand that your tasting the water is breaking a commitment to our valued clients?"

"Uhh."

"People depend on us to provide them with healthy, hygienic water. I don't know if you know this, but the UN declared access to clean water a human right in 2010."

The TV stayed frozen on the image of me with my tongue extended to taste the water drop on my finger. "We take our commitment to pure and clean water very seriously."

I waited for him to hurry up and fire me so I could walk out and figure out what I would do next.

Instead he said, "There are laws against what you've done. In 2020 Congress passed the Water Terrorism Act." He enunciated each word that came next. "You are a water terrorist."

I blinked back surprise.

"As such, the Dream Corporation has no choice but to prosecute you for your crime. Thank you for coming in today. Please allow our caretakers to show you to your cell."

For some reason, the only thing I was allowed to eat as a prisoner of the Dream Corporation was bananas. Always bananas, like I was a fucking chimpanzee. Every day they changed my water and handed me a cluster of bananas. I had no idea I could grow to hate bananas. The water they gave me wasn't the same as what I'd been harvesting, either. This was the regular water, the dirty water I was used to.

I grew accustomed, too, to my imprisonment. There was a television, and I left it on all day. I didn't think about the future. Part of me believed I would stay in this cell forever. Or as long as there was a forever.

But one morning as I was midway through my third or fourth banana of the day, the guard came by and announced that I had a visitor. It was Sun Myung himself, dressed in an expensive-looking suit with a tightly knotted skinny black tie.

He strode into the small hallway in front of my cell, glanced at me, then told the guard, "Take her to the visiting den."

The guard handcuffed me as he led me out of the cell. The metal felt cold against my wrists.

The visitor's den was nicer than I expected. Sun removed his glasses and polished them with a cloth from his pocket before he spoke.

 "Prisoner 21470," he said. "What's your name?" His accent was more pronounced than I remembered from his speeches on television.

"Hoda."

"Ho-dah," he repeated, breaking it apart like it was two short words.

"Did you grow up here? Egypt?"

"No, Kuwait."

"I see."

"Was your family wealthy?"

"Not very. Not compared to the Arabs."

"Your English is very good. Attend American school?"

I nodded.

"My children too." He laughed. "Their English is much better than mine."

I didn't know if this were an interrogation in which I was only supposed to answer questions or a conversation where I got to ask them too.

"Are you comfortable here? Are you getting enough food?"

I thought of my daily haul of bananas. "Yes."

Pleasantries out of the way, Sun cleared his throat and took a deep breath. "Why did you decide to drink Dream Corporations water?"

Unlike my first interrogator, Sun waited for a response.

"I wanted to taste it. To see if it still tasted like I remembered." I joggled my wrists, trying to find a comfortable position in the handcuffs.

"Water is a human right," Sun said, then met my gaze. "By drinking Dream Corporation's water without being a subscriber, you stole that water."

"It was just a taste," I tried.

He looked at me again, and seemed to decide there was no hope of reformation for me. "The quantity is unimportant."

I realized I had played this all wrong. I should have thrown myself at his feet and begged forgiveness, not shrugged and failed to acknowledge that I'd committed a heinous crime. But it was too late.

Sun pressed his lips together in a semblance of a smile and nodded a goodbye. His shoes clicked along the laminated floor as he walked away.

My trial lasted half an hour, mainly because Sun Myung's lawyer had a flair for the dramatic and wanted to deliver his rehearsed speech in its entirety. The verdict was as expected.

I didn't contact my family. What was the point? We were all having untimely demises. It was just our bad luck. Mine just happened to be three months earlier than everyone else's. Maybe it was better that way. I would be spared that last rush, all the effort and worry and stress.

I recited the fatiha.

Sun Myung, Adel, and a bunch of Sun's lawyers and representatives were in attendance for the execution.

The administrator wore polyester white pants with a white half-sleeved V-neck. Even his sneakers were white and unbranded. He was handsome, clean shaven, his hair thick and dark. He smiled at me and whispered, "Ready?"

I nodded. He rolled my shirt sleeve up. I barely felt the needle slide in. Then everything was white.

ANIMAL APOCALYPSE

Robert Duncan Gray

First came the snakes, then the jokes. The laughter was followed by horses and house cats. Labradors foaming at the mouth. The ocean opened its arms. The jungles shook their exotic birds into the sky. Finally, death.

This Apocalypse will not be televised. The enemy is among us. We, the Humans. They, the Animals. Our judgment arrives the day the beasts fight back. Having endured centuries of torture. Having been beaten, murdered and eaten. Cooked rotisserie style, baked and boiled. Microwaved, toasted and roasted. Having been leashed, lassoed and locked up. Having been walked. Having been pruned. The circus. The foxhunt. The barbeque. The ants under the magnifying glass. The salt on the slug. The fur coat. The lab rat. The hunt.

Their collective organization was inevitable. We should have seen it coming. Correction: We should have seen something coming. We could never have possibly predicted what came.

The snakes grew wings. The cat's scratch evolved poison. The sharks left the waters, slithered over land like sidewinders. The dogs, rabid with revenge, turned on their masters, biting the hand that feeds into a useless nub. The only necessary motivation was a thirst for blood. The zoos trembled and buckled under the pressure. The elephant stampeded downtown. The leopards perched over the pavement, waiting. The shrieks of monkeys, the roar of the gorilla. The lions' calm approach. The fight was over before it had begun.

How did the hummingbirds know to go straight for the eyes?

How did the wasps find the jugular vein?

The pigs stood proud behind the front line, watching from a strategic vantage point above the battle, directing waves of violence with the flick of a snout, nodding to one another in approval with an air of arrogance they could have only learned from a human.

six DEMONS

This new world was a vicious, sleek world made of street lights and tight jeans, sharp smiles and fast cars. This was a city, edited. A city, pared down to its bare minimums, beautiful and abusive.

—MAGGIE STIEFVATER

HOW WE BECOME WHAT WE BECOME

Evelyn Sharenov

J eff's mother's thin parchment-white wrist is tattooed with a row of small black numbers. I pester Jeff for an explanation when we play on the swings.

"Everyone's got them," he says.

"My parents don't have them. So not everyone's got them."

"They're lucky. So stop asking me."

We compete for who can launch the farthest from the highest arc of the swing. Then we tumble and tussle and walk home together to our neighboring apartments in the Bronx.

Jeff's mother joins my pantheon of great interests, supplants ancient Egypt and dinosaurs. During the hot High Holy Days in September, I stare at rows of wrists in temple, until my mother pokes me on my bare arm. She finally explains about the camps and Hitler.

I listen in on my parents' conversations. There's usually some tidbit about me. I'm pressed into the carpet just outside their door.

"It's not a healthy obsession," my mother says. "I don't want her to find out that Hazel locks Jeff in his room every night."

"She doesn't need to know that," my father agrees.

It's years before I work up the nerve to ask Jeff about this.

We spend our afternoons on Jeff's bed, doing homework. Hazel and Jack own a soda fountain and the school kids go there for egg creams after class. My mother teaches piano in our apartment, so we hang out at Jeff's.

Jeff's been begging me to touch him.

"I'll touch you if you answer a question."

Jeff rolls his eyes.

"Does your mother lock you in your room when you go to bed?"

"Yes."

"Why?"

"She's afraid someone will take me. I had a brother and sister. They were killed by the Nazis."

"But what if you have to pee?"

"I knock on the wall and they let me out."

I'm good to my word and touch him. He puts his hand on mine and shows me how to hold on. Then he moans and springs a leak. He touches my panties then sniffs. When he puts his fingers under my cotton panties, he strokes something that sets off firecrackers through my belly and down my thighs. Jeff kisses me with soft damp lips.

"You're very pretty," he says.

"Go practice," my mother says, but Mozart's 16th piano sonata is the last thing on my mind. What's between my legs takes first place in the pantheon of great interests.

"Stop tickling the ivories," she calls from the kitchen.

Jeff and I commute to different colleges. He's pre-med at Hofstra and I'm prepping for Juilliard. He parks his car and I emerge from the subway onto the Grand Concourse about the same time each day.

"Can I come over?" he asks. "I listen to you practice. It's beautiful." I keep the windows open when I play.

He takes a spoon, a needle, a lighter, a tourniquet and a packet of powder from his canvas bookbag.

"Do you mind if I do this here?"

His father's been dead two years and their store is gone. We have no place else to go.

I watch him inject heroin into a vein behind his right knee. He pulls the syringe out before it's all gone.

"I saved a little for you."

He strokes my skin. I barely feel the needle prick. Before I go under, I wonder if his mother still locks him in his room at night. Then Jeff's inside me and I love him and I leave that other world for the moments he's with me.

MYPOCOLYPSE

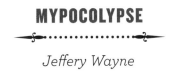

Jeffery Wayne

I've wet the bed again. Eight years old, I wish I could stop.

I need my hunting knife. I take it from the dresser drawer. Slide it out of its leather sheath, turn it over and over in my hand and remind myself how it feels. I slide my thumb across the business edge. Still sharp. I place it back in the sheath, lay it carefully on the empty bed.

I should tell the others again, but nobody believes me. They never will.

I need six feet of high-test fishing line. In my tackle box in the closet I find some 25lb test line. It should work fine. It doesn't have to take the full weight, just a little bit. For only a moment. A glorious moment. The fishing line takes its place on the bed next to the knife.

Why are people so dumb? So numb? Yet a kid like me is nothing but lies? Apparently.

Finally, I'll need two one inch wood screws and a Phillips screwdriver. I find all three in my toolbox and then place them on the bed along with the knife and the fishing line.

I might have lied once or twice about silly things like cookies swiped after bed or homework lost, not finished. But not about something this important.

I look over the items on the bed. Go over my plan. I must stay focused. It won't do to worry about the consequences. Everyone will be better off.

I take the items and place them in a knapsack. The clock says 1:13 a.m.

I remove my shoes and quietly ascend the first flight of stairs to the top. I crack the door. No light. No sound of the 24-hour news from the television. I slip out into the hall and around the corner to the stairs leading up to the main bedroom.

I crawl on my hands and knees, one step every few seconds, to the top. I wait there, not breathing, listening for any signs of wakefulness. After a few minutes I am convinced now is the time.

I remove one screw and the driver from the sack. I slowly turn a screw into the banister about six inches above the floor. I remove the second screw and turn it into the wall directly across from the banister.

I place the screwdriver back into the sack and remove the fishing line. I make a fisherman's slipknot and loop it around the head of the screw in the banister. I pull the line and wrap it four times around the opposite screw, and tie a fisherman's hook knot around it. I place the remaining line back into the sack and withdraw the knife. I carefully trim the excess line off each side and place the knife back into the sack.

The line is nice and tight. Strong. Just the right height. Invisible.

Back down the first set of stairs, through the hall, and quietly down into my basement room. It smells of urine, as always. That will change.

I sit on the dry edge of the bed and wait. How could he get it so wrong? Why didn't somebody stop him. If they had, I wouldn't have to. A kid. It's no job for a kid.

He always gets up to get a drink of whiskey around 3 a.m. because he can't sleep. No surprise.

Forty-five minutes. I replay all of the yelling, hitting, threatening, in my head. I roll it around my mind like something that doesn't belong to me. He'll take it with him.

I start to nod off but am shaken awake by a sound. The sound of my plan coming together. The sound of a my pain being carried away from me. The sound of my problem tumbling down the stairs.

Soon after sirens. Yelling. Crying. Screaming. I wait quietly in my room. They come.

They ask me why. All of them. They don't seem angry. They just don't understand. They want to know if I hold the secret to some ageless mystery. Maybe I do.

A tear slips from my eye. I turn my gaze to each of them.

And I answer.

I don't want to wet the bed anymore.

LA FLACA

Tod McCoy

Suelita, my horse, stumbled as I spurred her on and she nearly threw me into the rocky hillside. I had forced us too far into the desert in July and knew that one of us probably wouldn't make it back to Tucson. I'd misjudged the morning clouds. The water in my canteen was nearly gone.

I looked for a shady place to die. Perhaps one day my sister's children would find me here, the body of their prospecting tio, hidden among the Santa Catalinas. Would they know I came out here looking for Jesuit gold, looking for some redemption? Doubtful. I only hoped they wouldn't make the same mistakes that I had, and that they would never taunt the desert.

The heat of the rocks and the fragrant sage rose in the summer sun. I dropped from Suelita and pulled us into the shade of a rocky outcropping, glad of the tiniest breeze. I sat, and reached my hand up to my horse's hot nose.

It was then a shadow passed in front of me. A figure. A human. I stood and looked up above the outcropping: a girl, maybe ten or twelve, gazing down at me, the corona of the sun flaring around her hair, a transfigured image of humanity. I did not believe in religion, even though my mother did. Apparition or not, I was glad to speak to someone.

"I'm lost," I said. "I'm almost out of water and my phone is out of range. I don't have a car and it's sixty miles to Tucson. Can you help?"

She had dark hair, tanned skin, wore a sleeveless shirt and pants made of hemp or some other coarse material, scraps sewn together with some measure of skill. She watched me as if the sun had no effect on her. But I had grown up here, too, after the Dissolution of the United States, and at one time I could handle the heat as well as she. "Can you help? Ayuda, por favor?" She turned and disappeared. "Wait! Don't go yet!"

No one lived around here for dozens of miles, not since the energy wars decimated Arizona. Our family made some money raising horses and mining, but resources were getting scarce. The world turned its back on the desert and left us for dead. I read somewhere about the legend of the Jesuit-buried gold, the Iron Door legend, and I had to find it, even if it killed me.

My father disappeared one day doing the same thing. Find some wood, my mother would frown and say. You can't burn gold. My tia called it en busca de sus ojos, and shook her head.

I did not want to die so easily. It was not in my blood. I thought the girl abandoned me but heard a tumble of rocks and then saw a blur of motion as she slipped on the rocky embankment, falling several feet, just missing a cholla and landing on her side with a hoomph. She looked at her bloody, scraped palms, and scrambled to her feet as I approached. I could see her face now. A girl, and like most of us around here, a blend of Mexican, European, Indian, African, whatever else was left alive. Maybe a little Papago. Her skin pockmarked and parched from a short life in the sun.

"So you're not a diablita," I said. "Are you hurt?"

She hesitated for a moment, then crawled under a large boulder, so that I could see only her elbow.

"Come out and let me have a look at you."

She didn't move.

"Entiendes? I am not a bad man."

Nothing.

"Are you from New California. Maybe you're a spy from the Kingdom of Texas? Or Mexico?" She didn't laugh, but I hoped it amused her.

"Water?" I unhooked my canteen. "I have almost none left. But it's yours."

Her body shifted and her head poked out. I could see the gleam of desire in her eyes as she crawled from under the boulder. She took the canteen and drank the rest, a treat sweeter than candy, despite the fact you could brew tea from its warmth.

Blood dripped where her shirt had been torn.

"Don't move. Let me have a look."

As she drank, I lifted the edge of her shirt a little and could see the wide, dirty scrape just above her hip. Flaca, I thought, she is so skinny she had nothing but bones to cushion her fall. It reminded me of an old tale my tia told me about a skinny woman who appears to people just before their death. La Flaca. The skinny girl. Mala diosa Diabla.

My hand trembled a little at the thought.

"You need to put some medicine on that." She still said nothing. I brushed the dirt out of the wound and she swatted my hands away. She walked down the slope to Suelita and looked at the horse's face. My legs ached. Dizziness crawled across my eyes.

I remembered something else my tia said to me. When faced with Death, talk to it. Tell it a story. Keep yourself alive, because Death will listen to stories.

"I'm looking for something," I said. I tried to sit and fell to the ground. "Maybe you've seen it." I didn't like to tell my tale. I wanted to keep it to myself, but facing death changed my mind.

"There's an old, old tale. Very old. Way before the oil wars. Way before they knew what oil was. Some priests were driven out by some other priests, because holy men can only be violent to other holy men. Before they left they buried their gold. They covered it with an iron door to keep it safe. They were going to come back for it later, but they never did. This was long before the war that tore apart the United States.

People have been looking for it for centuries. Have you seen an iron door in the ground?"

She stroked Suelita's face and finished off my canteen, offering the last drops to the horse before tossing the empty container aside.

I dragged myself a few feet, to a point where I could look across the valley. Far, far away, across the flat desert floor toward the ruins of North Tucson, lay the solar fields. Nothing more than a glint of sunlight in the distance.

My tia would be riding her bicycle among them, taking midday temperature readings, sweating in the summer sun, earning enough to keep us fed. I closed my eyes and listened as the insects chirruped, busy with their day, and the heat climbed.

With a groan and a wheeze, Suelita toppled over, her mouth frothing. I couldn't move, couldn't comfort the horse, because I knew in short order I would be there myself.

Unmoved by the animal's plight, the girl laughed, a high pitched giggle. A laugh that pierced the sky and reached into the ages. She turned and looked at me, but I could see no sympathy. Only darkness in her eyes.

The world I knew was dying, too, and it seemed as if an old order was reasserting itself.

"Are you here to take my life?"

She smiled, and her grin spread wider than her head, her mouth opened impossibly large, stretching from horizon to horizon, and she vanished.

The horse kicked once, and was dead. Prospecting, I thought, a futile art. Now I knew what my father knew.

"If you find the iron door, La Flaca" I called out, "don't you tell anyone where it is."

I knew she wouldn't.

BIOCHEMICAL WEAPON ZOMBIE DOG DREAM:
A POLITICAL ALLEGORY

Yu-Han Chao

A fast-moving escalator takes me downstairs in a blindingly white train station. On my way down, I see a suspicious-looking man riding the escalator up, carrying a large, ticking device in a cardboard box. I immediately rush to tell a security guard about the man, and he tells me to run out of the building, fast as I can. People look at me like I'm crazy, fleeing as I am for my life and gesturing for everyone to follow me.

"Get out while you can!" I yell.

Beyond the train station, there are tall buildings in every direction. It's difficult running in a straight line—I have to avoid the buildings and wait to cross busy intersections where cars zoom by, fighting over who gets to flatten me. I eventually run through the gates of a school because there's no way around it. Some students congregate in a classroom; breathless, I tell them about the bomb in the train station. We all pile into a van together and plan to drive as far away as possible. What the hell do we care about speed limits now?

As we drive we see a group of children running in one direction, and some adults running in another. There are packs of violent, rabid zombie dogs chasing them. We realize that the bomb was actually a biochemical weapon that transformed dogs into man-eating zombies. As we drive on, outside the car windows dogs are tearing people apart with sharp canine teeth right before our eyes.

FIRST ENDING

I ask the person driving the vehicle to run over some of the zombie dogs but he swerves every time to avoid them. Finally, we're cornered, and he has to run over one, two, and a few more of the dogs, who are foaming at the mouth, teeth sharp and gleaming. A man kills one of the strongest looking dogs, the pack leader, and seeing that their leader has been massacred, the remaining dogs suddenly become quiet and submissive. We wish we had started killing the dogs earlier, before they ate as many people as they did. Now we'll have to rebuild civilization.

But it's a new society. Here, minorities have all the privileges because they came into power first. Everything, including technology, is very advanced; there is no racism, there are no immigration problems, and no healthcare debates.

SECOND ENDING

This time, a woman kills the rabid zombie dog pack leader, lopping its head off with a clean chop. Finally, women rule the world. I feel very happy here. There is no more sexism, no more rapists, no more workplace discrimination. Women make more money than men, and are the heads of their households.

THIRD ENDING

I witness a tall, Caucasian man murder the pack leader with his bare hands. Not just the witnesses who were there, but all the people of the world are in awe of his strength. As a result of his coming into power, the world is rebuilt in its own pre-apocalyptic image, an elitist and racist place where minorities are oppressed and technology lags.

AFTER THE VERY FIRST QUIET MORNING

Jolie Mandelbaum

Because no one was left to protect me, I relied on the cats to sniff out potential people. They used to say (I don't know who They are, and anyway, They are probably stains now since it seems like They would work in high rise buildings), but They used to say that animals can see into hearts, which is how they knew whose feet to sit near at dinner to get the most scraps.

With no new ways being invented to solve problems, you rely on the old, true or not.

When I first moved here, I hated this basement. I hated everything about it, except for the rent, which was half what I was paying before and I was ready to suffer any injustice to save that much money a month. The rest of the house was built on a hill and the basement was sunk into the ground with steps that led down to my door.

My friends had good jobs and lived in the high-rises. I dreamed of those apartments, with their slick wood floors and swaying balconies, the microwaves that beeped when finished and the LEDs would flash ENJOY YOUR MEAL. I'd have killed someone for appliances that spoke to me and trash chutes in the hallway. I looked at floorplans the way other people looked at porn or Vogue, with that painful sense of longing.

Those friends are dead now—they've been dead a good six months. Melted into those slick wood floors, I bet, just like the woman who owns (owned) this house. Her stain is in the kitchen upstairs. I walk around her. It only seems right. I had a boyfriend in another city up until the day I found all the spiders dead in their webs, and I'd be upset if someone walked on his stain. He lived in one of those nice apartments, too. He moved out of DC for work, promised to come back for me, signed a lease on a beautiful apartment in Sarasota. He's melted like my friends. I accept that.2.All the houses on my block were built on the side of a hill like my house, all the basements turned into cheap rental units. The homeowners are stains. The renters lived. There are stains outside, too. The melted outside cats disturb me the most, and when I come home, I always make sure to pick up Bad and Worse and give them hugs and extra cat food.

The first week, no one left their houses. I had food for a month and the power still worked, so I hadn't panicked yet. Still, I knew that being a city slicker was a serious disadvantage. I majored in humanities in college and knew how to think, how to analyze art. I knew how to throw pottery and I knew which plays were better live. I knew how to tip waitstaff and what kind of manicure was appropriate for a business dinner. I knew about sexism and rape culture and how the media plays on every fault we have as human beings to sell us face cream and cars and beautiful apartments with shining floors.

These skills are useless now; philosophy is a thing of the past. I had useful friends who knew what parts of a whole animal were actually the edible ones. I had friends who knew how to bait a fishing line, friends who could fix anything mechanical and who could make engines sing. I had friends who could grow their own gardens, friends who could go out into any wooded area and find wild mustard, friends who knew if the water was clean, friends who could kill things.

They all lived in the high rises. They are stains and the little art critic lives. Every time I think about it, I laugh. Especially since I'm eating boxes of mac and cheese I stole from the Safeway and I've yet to stab a fish with a sharpened stick. The cats don't even hunt. Even during the end of the world, my cats and I live like good Americans, sitting on the sofa and eating food out of boxes.3.On the Very First Quiet Morning (I've been trying to come up with a name, and I think that's a good one), the internet and cell phones went. I didn't even try to get to work—cars full of stains blocked the road. I was smart enough to see that I'd never make another student loan payment as long as I lived. Fuck you, Sallie Mae. I won.

A week and a day after the Very First Quiet Morning, the power went out and the basement door to the house across the street opened. Lou walked out holding a marijuana pipe in one hand and his flip flops in the other. Lou had lived in that basement for years and I'd met him before the Quiet Morning. He was a back-up guitar player in a local band and a smalltime drug dealer, mostly pot and chocolate laced with peyote. He had a receding hairline and a penchant for plaid shorts. Lou threw his flip flops on the ground, stepped into them, walked over to my door, and knocked. Both cats took off for the kitchen. I opened the front door and Lou and I climbed up the concrete steps into the front yard. There was a stain in the shape of a squirrel on the side of one tree and a stain in the shape of a bird on the grass.Lou lit the pipe and handed it to me; I breathed in deep and handed it back. The protocol, it seemed, remained the same.

"So," he said.

"Are we it?" I asked.

"I don't think so," he said.

"What happened?"

"I don't know. I woke up and shit was all fucked up. But I've seen the basement curtains moving this week; I know we're in there."

I said, "My friends and I used to play at the zombie apocalypse. We used to fetishize the end of the world. We did this for fun. We'd run from the remnants of humanity and then we'd get drunk and camp. Post-apoc was a genre."

Lou went to the next basement apartment and I followed him, still pulling from the pipe. He seemed disinterested in my philosophical musings about living my hobby. The burning in my throat was delicious and I started to feel light headed, airy, a little giggly. I stopped noticing stains. I hummed the chorus to a song I didn't know anymore.

Lou and I collected ten renters—seven men and three women, and everyone met in Lou's backyard. We decided that, since the homeowners were all stains and the food in the garage freezers was going to go bad, we should smoke the rest of Lou's pot and have a pit BBQ.

The men went into each garage and dragged any edible meat down to the street while the women piled up branches. A married couple walked to the grocery store and returned with 4 carts, which we broke apart and used as grates to lay over the fire. I threw the steaks over the hot slats and smoked more. I ate the meat partially raw and then smoked more.

Someone found potatoes in a root cellar and threw them on the carts. I ate those and smoked more. Someone else raided a wine cellar. I lay back on the street and thought, "This isn't too bad."

When I woke up, everyone was asleep in the street except for Lou, who had walked into our houses, gathered up anything he found useful, put it in a shopping cart and, I suppose, headed off to try his luck.

I took the stairs into the main house, walking carefully around the landlady stain. Then I took a cue from Lou and packed everything useful and brought it downstairs. I wouldn't have to look at her stain anymore. Every day became Saturday. I woke up, fed the cats, grabbed my backpack, and walked on the trails to keep my muscles ready to carry me away. I'd take the park trails into different sections of town, go into grocery stores, take what I needed, and walk back. It would be a long time before I exhausted the grocery stores. Most of the basement dwellers took off to find their families. I wished them good luck. I didn't bother. My mother and grandmother had above-ground apartments just like my boyfriend. These are the things I realized the first day.

I estimated that maybe 75 percent of the world had been knocked out—anyone who lived in a major city. There were more than enough of us left to fix things and surely a builder or a farmer or an engineer lived. I wondered why no one had shown up, or why the army wasn't deployed to find survivors.

When I played end-of-the-world, I pictured myself as a hero, blowing down doors, hotwiring trucks, climbing fences with a kicky band of adventurers. But here I don't matter. There is no massive search for me; my band of adventurers will not find out that whatever happened was a government conspiracy. I will not be hunted down for knowing too much. I will not be leading the people in a glorious revolution. I will not be shooting two guns at the same time. There will be no last stand inside the Governor's Mansion.

I'm eating boxed rice and reading books, flinching when I see child-shaped stains, and I won't move into the main house because what if whatever happened happens again. 5.Another woman who lived in the neighborhood knocked on my door one day, though I didn't know when that was, or even what season. The cats scattered and I answered anyway. She introduced herself as "from next door" and I let her in.

She had a face that looked like it was slowly slipping off and I realized that for the first time in my life, I was conventionally beautiful. Or I would be, if there was still such a thing as convention. Since ice cream no longer existed, I was no longer chubby, and the walks had tanned me and toned my legs. My hair had grown out brown and was wild around me, though there was enough conditioner at the abandoned CVS to keep it untangled for years.

She said, "Do you have any tampons?"

I said, "Oh, no, but the landlady did. They're all upstairs." Truth be told, since it was just me, I often just bled all over what I was wearing. After bathing in a lake and coming out covered in algae, hygiene no longer seemed so important, though I wondered how long it would be before my teeth started breaking.

She looked me up and down again and then backed away. Her old lady haircut was growing out and framed her face in uneven layers. I reached forward and touched her hair, which felt like unfurling twine.

She turned for the door and said "Well, my husband and I are going to try and find my sister…" Then she turned and was gone.6.It was daybreak when I heard pounding on the door. I sat up in bed, listened hard, and then calculated how much the door could hold. Bad and Worse began scratching and meowing and I cursed the little traitors for letting someone know I was in here.

I slipped out of bed and pulled on a pair of pants and a destroyed Slayer t-shirt. Then I crept into the kitchen and picked up two cast iron frying pans.

I tiptoed to the door and both cats bolted for the bathroom. I put my ear against the wood and listened.

"Izzy, Izzy," I heard spoken right into the wood, like the speaker had his lips pressed up against the unfinished knots. "Iz, be in there."

I used to think that hearing a flashbulb go off when you figured something out was a myth. I opened the door and there stood my faraway boyfriend, thinner and hoarse-voiced, but unmistakably him, down to the scars lacing his forearms that I used to trace when he slept next to me. I dropped the frying pans and they made a horrific noise.

He said, "Hello."

He said, "I walked."

He said, "You look tan and a bit tired."

He said, "I missed you."

I stood back from him and he crossed the threshold. I crossed my arms over my chest and didn't say anything. It's happened, I thought. I'm hallucinating. The human mind can only take so much.

He said, "I bet you thought I was dead."

He said, "I slept that night in my car, in the underground parking garage at work, so I could get up and go right back in for launch."

He said, "Can I sit down?"

I gestured him over to the sofa and sat down next to him. He radiated body heat and I knew he was real. It had been so long, I didn't think to hug him; I got up and got him a bottle of warm water from the kitchen. When I returned I stood in front of him as he sat on the sofa and leaned into him. His hand spanned my lower back and he said, "You smell good, like salt and sunscreen."

I said, "Do you know what happened?"

"No, not really. I didn't walk up here to kick down the door to the White House. Some bomb went off, some disease, but it must have been a little one since we lived. No one is in the cities. Everyone left went to the middle of nowhere, where they thought it was safer."

I climbed off him and pulled a bag of potato chips off the bookshelf. I asked him if he wanted me to pack up the cats and head to the country, though I didn't see how I was going to get the cats there.He said, "Well, things seem to be working out here for you, we could stay here for a while."

So we will.

SPITEFUL COMPANION

Deb Scott

I am afraid of a lot of things. I am afraid of what can be seen and what can't. I'm afraid of the end of the world, or at least the world as we know it. I'm afraid we will push the earth beyond its ability to maintain us, maybe we already have. Rivers are running red but I don't believe it is from the wrath of some mythical patriarch in the sky. I think rather our own misjudgments and arrogance will bring the end of our times. I'm more afraid of extremist ideologies hiding out in honest churches, synagogues, mosques, and natural places of peaceful reflection taking the soul of a belief and turning it, with mal intent towards hatred and fear. I'm afraid my children's children will be doomed by our current unwillingness to lovingly accept and honor 'the other'. We will surely kill ourselves with malice, mistrust, and greed. I'm afraid if we are not careful and wise, we will be the Armageddon. Fear is my spiteful companion. It demands my allegiance and then hounds me with the most damaging inner dialogue."You are so stupid.""What an idiot you are.""Quit acting like a child.""Aren't you ashamed of yourself?" "You are stupid, stupid, stupid."The litany goes on and on. I am afraid of imagined threats and real, true scary things that deserve a full dose of fear. But my fear is not very selective, nor does it relent. As young as five years old I was regularly watching "The Twilight Zone", "The Outer Limits" and "Alfred Hitchcock Presents", so my fear pump was primed for psychological terrors that would come from real life run ins with evil in the form of human behavior. One episode of "Alfred Hitchcock" in particular had me screaming for weeks every time I looked in a mirror. I was afraid I would be dragged into the hellish world on the other side, trapped forever like the people on TV.And then there were the Saturday movie fears. I was okay with some of those films. "The Blob" didn't scare me, nor did most of the space alien movies. I felt sorry for Godzilla and Rodan. I didn't like the films with giant radioactive bugs. "Dracula" and "Dr. Sardonicus" had me closing my eyes and putting my fingers in my ears. I'm still terrified of bats.The most terrifying films for me though were mostly Japanese productions that involved earthquakes. This was unfortunate as I grew up in Southern California, earthquake central. In these films, the earth would open up in large jagged lines splintering earth and families with no regard. People who only moments before were doing their usual day to day tasks suddenly fell into the gaping mouth where a sidewalk had been and then, Wham! The earth would slam shut again and some person who was inches away from release would scream as the world crushed them in a horrifying death. My family tried to soothe me but it never occurred to them to turn off the TV or watch something different while I was in the room. And they didn't know I had already had personal contact with the devil in the form of a teenager in a park bathroom, an adult babysitter's demented adult brother, my own family members. I never told about these 'Twilight Zone' or 'Outer Limits' experiences until I was an adult, I had so adeptly hidden them away from my own consciousness, a useful survival tactic and one children learn well. Unfortunate the child mind is unable to decipher the tricky differences between real and unreal. The magic of imagination contains both dark and light.

As a parent of two adult children I now wonder with dread how much fear

I may have passed on to my sons. I think back on times when I could not contain my heart pounding anxieties. I think they think I am weak and skittish, and I guess this is partially true. What they couldn't know and I couldn't tell them was my concern was for their very lives, that my fear demanded they avoid those things that terrified me. At some point I became paralyzed by thunder and lightning. My first husband's young cousin who I met two years before his death was struck and killed in a lightning storm while standing on the family porch holding his father's hand. When my sons were young and their dad took them out on our porch, I begged him to bring them inside. He brushed away my fear like a nagging fly and stood there with them counting the seconds between vibrating boom and sky shattering light. I huddled on the staircase sobbing, unable to move, unable to believe they would be okay, furious that their dad didn't heed my warning of the young dead boy.

One winter we had a wind storm so ferocious that even my husband was concerned. The power had been knocked out and I stood at the windows of my children's bedrooms watching as huge trees, forest grown and hardy, whirled in circles looking as though they may be unscrewed from the earth and fly through the air targeting the house. I insisted we bundle the kids up and take them to the basement. We made a game of it, camping in the house while the lights were out. As they all slept, I kept the watch, wandering from room to room and up and down the stairs all night until the wind finally subsided. My fear took much longer to calm. I had to stop going with my family to get our annual Christmas tree. I am afraid of bears and cougars and when walking in the woods my husband had the unforgivable habit of heading off so fast that I could never keep up. One time he had my oldest son and I was carrying the youngest, still almost a baby. Alone in the woods all the noises became those of predators. I wept my way back to the car. By the time my husband and son returned I was inconsolable, certain they had been attacked, my lovely son torn to pieces. In order to allow the experience to be enjoyable for my kids, I just didn't go anymore. The same became true of camping.But my deepest fear for my sons was that they too would experience the invasions of body and soul that had permeated my childhood. I didn't know how to turn off the suspicious radar that every person had to pass through before they could have access to my children. When out of my sight with their friends I would have full blown panic attacks. I worked hard in therapy to learn how to keep these fears to myself, to allow my sons to grow up without my shadows haunting every part of their lives. This is still a work in progress but I think they now have a better understanding, I think they know I desperately wanted them to be safe. I hope they forgive the times it felt or looked crazy.I am still afraid of earthquakes and tornadoes. I am afraid of bears and cougars and bats in my bedroom. I'm afraid of spiders and snakes. I'm afraid of a certain part of the road I drive every day because I am sure the whole rock face will one day fall on me as I am driving by. I'm afraid of passing big trucks on the Interstate. I am afraid of dying by someone's misdirected hate. I am afraid of making a fool of myself, of speaking my mind, of looking or sounding stupid. I am afraid of many things. Mostly now though, I am afraid of not being known for who I really am. I'm afraid I will die with my truth still untold.

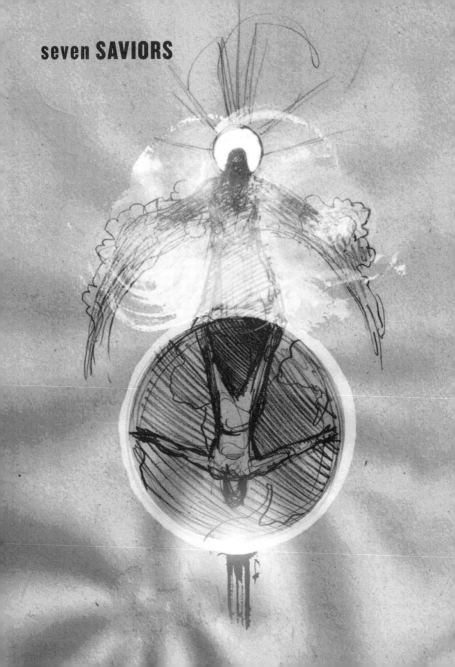

seven **SAVIORS**

Human beings will be happier, not when they cure cancer or get to Mars, but when they find ways to inhabit primitive communities again.

—KURT VONNEGUT

THE PEN

Carrie Seitzinger

The way I see it, there are now only two ways to live. When we are happy, and the women are sweet, with stomachs like cutting boards, and the boys are young Adam's apples, and the joy of our lives fills us and we are not compelled to move so much as lay around, or stare off at something lovely, not thinking at all how lovely it is, not thinking much at all. In this life, we roll over the earth because it is the same on our backs as on our bellies.

We hold the pen above paper

And forget why

Because we know

We have nothing to say.

Then there is the way to live where we are terrified, uncomfortable, and the women will not be mothers or even pretend to harness the hobgoblin or the real animal monsters, and the boys drool more each night, and their cries arrest the head, pack the ears like infection, and the nights grow so large that they howl and snarl and the stars are no longer pinpricks but shining fangs pointing downward. In this life, we pound our fists, frightened by what is coming, too misshapen to rest on each side of our bodies, afraid of our unevenness. When the wisest has gone and hidden all of the pens, because when we get our hands on them we are the most expansive fury. If we get a chance, our hands are the blades of jackhammers, mining ourselves into our graves that others can fall down.

Each day we choose which life to live.

Either the bliss that drills a hole in our torsos,

Leaking the art and words we have to say,

Or the torture that hardens over us like an eggshell,

Our writing hands weaker than the embryo's beak,

We are trying to break apart,

We are trying to write our way out of this.

REVOLUTION

Mai'a Williams

The sun rarely comes out. And when it does the six-inch window at the top of the Brooklyn basement apartment only produces the shadows and whispers of sunlight. Dishes are piled in the sink. There's a bottle of bodega liquor in the middle of the table next to a two-liter bottle of Sprite. The Mis-education of Lauryn Hill plays on the stereo. Raye and I sit at the small plastic table in Raye's apartment while Dani cooks spinach tofu and noodles on the stove. Next to Raye is a little wooden pipe and a neon pink lighter. A stick of cheap incense sticks out of a crack in the wall, the ashes fall into an empty glass.

"Oh shit," Dani says. "I poured hot water into the pot."

Raye turns around. "So what?"

"The water doesn't boil as fast if you put in hot water."

"That doesn't make any sense. Hot water would boil faster than cold."

Dani, Raye, and I went to college together and were the co-chairs of the Black Radical Congress on our campus. On Juneteenth, we took a 12-hour bus ride to Chicago and spent three days falling in and out of love (and bed) with black radicals from around the world.

Dani graduated last spring and works as an office temp. Last year, Raye and I volunteered with the Black Panther Collective in Harlem. She is taking second semester of her second year off, working in retail and studying the lessons of Allah. I, too, am taking some time off from our northeast private college.

Dani dumps the hot water down the drain. I shiver looking at her copper back slouching over the sink. In the winter, I wear three layers to her one. She gave up working strip clubs a couple of months ago.

"I got burned out," she says when Raye asks why she quit.

Raye starts packing the bowl. "Yeah, if I don't get this phone company job soon, I was thinking of dancing in a club."

Raye's thick black locks fall in her doll face. She squints her almond eyes and reaches for the Zippo lighter she scored from her boyfriend. She has fallen in love with a god, a yellow pretty boy with dark green eyes, Prince Born Understanding. They started building a couple of months ago. And after much deep discussions and finger fucking, she reverted to full on five-percenter nation of gods and earths. Nowadays she dresses three-quarters covered, her locks wrapped like Erykah Badu's. She keeps Prince's cream-colored pistol, a god's version of a promise ring, behind her door.

First year of college Raye and I were the only two black girls on our floor. Her best friend and roommate, Lyndzee, was a blond girl from Jersey with red cheeks and a gospel voice. They both loved listening to R&B and hip hop, smoking weed, making out with street boys, and sipping rum and cokes before bed.

Life was bella until the night Lyndzee said, "Why black people be so lazy?" and Raye went off and started kicking the shit out of her. Lyndzee managed to crawl out of that dorm room with only a black eye, a bloody nose and a couple of small clumps of blond hair missing.

The next day I asked, "Raye, you punched her?"

"Yeah, I punched that bitch." Her left hand rubbed her right knuckle. "See, if she say something racist like that again."

You'd think from the swagger that Raye had grown up singing the inner city blues. But no, she was a south Jersey girl, graduated from a private school. Raye didn't care. The way she saw it was you were either with her or against her.

That fall I spent a couple of nights with her in Brooklyn. We were sitting at her table drinking tea and talking about her being in love.

"Look, at what he got me," she said as she pulled out a lipstick tube from her coat pocket. She took off the top and turned the bottom tube. Instead of lipstick, a metal blade rotated upward.

"Whoa." I said. "That shit is off the chain."

She handed it to me.

"Is it legal?"

She said. "It's just short enough that it's legal to carry concealed."

The blade was shaped like a softened zig-zag and nipped my skin like a paper cut as I rubbed it across my palm.

Raye took me to the apartment Prince shared with his crew. We drank rum and coke and hit a blunt or two. He started talking about the origins of whites living in caves in the Caucus Mountains.

"Oh," I said, "have you read about the archeological findings in Turkey, and the theories about goddess worship among early human civilizations?" Next thing I knew we were arguing about the naturalness of homosexuality.

"Once you knowledge one-twenty then you can understand that in our original natural state of being, men and women are supposed to be together."

I countered, "but how do you decide what is and what isn't natural? Isn't that more about our own interpretation of the natural world?"

"You can tell what is natural by looking at what happens in nature. You don't see no free male animals having sex with each other. They have sex to reproduce. That is natural."

No, I thought, there are plenty of examples of homosexuality in the 'wild,' but fuck it, I was already getting dirty looks from his boys.

A few weeks later, he was having a party with some kids from his studio who perpetually were 'just about to get signed.' Raye introduced me to a 'really deep sister' in a black dress and red head wrap who asked if I had read Giving Birth to the Nation. "It proves that it's healthiest for black women to have children in their late teens and early twenties."

I pipe up still a little buzzed off the trees Raye and I had smoked earlier, "I think I would rather adopt than have a biological children. The world is over populated as it is."

She clenched her jaw and curled her upper lip. "It is the duty of every righteous black family to have children. Over population is a myth that white people created as an excuse to continue the slaughter of the black people around the world."

Every morning Raye dutifully breaks down the day's supreme mathematics. "Today is January 4, 1999. One. Four. One represents knowledge, the foundation of all existence, for you have to know it to make it manifest. Knowledge is the sun which is the Original Man, the foundation of Allah's family. Knowledge equals sun equals the original people. And four represents culture and freedom, which means 'free-dome.' Have to have a free mind. And the way that you manifest free dome culture is to get your knowledge right, get your foundations right, because you can't have a culture with an ignorant people who do not recognize that they are the original people."

I look up from reading one of her pamphlets. "So the man is one is the sun, right?"

"Yeah."

"And woman is two is the moon."

"Yeah."

"And moon reflects the sun, the way the woman is supposed to reflect the man? But if the woman represents life, then shouldn't she be the sun and the man be the moon? Doesn't he just reflect her?"

"I never thought about it like that."

"Why is the man the god and the woman is the earth? If god created everything in the universe, that sounds like what women do. We are the creators. We give birth to life. Not men."

We spend hours memorizing and building on her 120 lessons and figuring out the supreme alphabet of what her new nation name would be. Queen Aliya Born Understanding. Khalilah Original Star. Moon Khadija Born Love? On her bookshelf, next to the Cornel West and Ntozake Shange that she had been reading last year when, stood thin blue spines. Allah's Teachings Revealed. The Prophecies of War in the Middle East. The Righteous Earth: Mother, Wife, Life.

Last year Raye had wanted to be a writer. Now her dream was to become a five-percenter, get a job at the phone company, and give birth to Prince's revolutionary black stars.

"Wait a second," Dani says, picking up the bowl and the lighter. "I don't understand what a five-percenter really is."

Raye leans over to the shelf and picks up a dog-eared book, The True

Origins of the White Man. "You see Dani," she starts, "you have to go back to the Bible."

A flame hits the edge of the bowl and Dani inhales.

I've heard this same speech a dozen times. I can recite it myself. In the beginning was the original black man and woman. And they reproduced. And created the wise and civilized black nation. White people are devils who were created in a laboratory by an evil scientist (it's in the Bible) and then the white people escaped from the lab and have been running wild ever since. But it has been prophesied that at the end of the 6,000 years the curse against black people will be lifted and every white person will be destroyed in an apocalyptic war. Thankfully, the year 2000 A.D. marks the end of the 6,000 year reign of white people. There are the 85 percent of people who see no truth, hear no truth, and speak no truth. There are 10 percent of the people who see the truth, and hear the truth, but refuse to speak the evil to the rest of the people, thus keeping them in ignorance, and using their ignorance to rule the world. Lastly, there are the five percent who see, hear, and speak the truth to the people in order to open their eyes.

Dani's eyes grow wide. "You don't actually believe that do you, Raye? You don't actually believe that all white people are evil?"

Raye leans back in her chair. "Yeah. I do. I think that white pig beating up poor black folks is a devil."

"But some white people are actually conscious. Some white people actually get it. Like Blu."

Raye looks at the white tiled floor. "Blu's cool and it's not her fault she's the devil. So yeah. That will be sad when she dies."

I pour another ghetto cocktail. "Blu would step in front of a bullet for you."

Blu is one of those suburban Jewish girls who blends in a posse of queer women of color even though she is chalky pale and looks like a pissed off 10-year-old boy. She'll yell at a guy three times her size and kick him in the balls with her kid's section combat boots for looking at her friends the wrong way.

"Raye," I say, "when the revolution comes a lot of white people may die, but Blu is down. She's on our side."

Dani looks at me. "Do you think this is true? I mean all this...this..." She waves her hand over Raye's books. "The Bible is just a bunch of made up stories, right?"

I shrug. "I believe in it about as much as I believe that cold water boils faster than hot water."

Raye looks at me, eyes wide. She gathers the empty dishes and puts them in the sink and runs hot water over them for a few seconds. Her arm brushes my cheek as she walks back to the table. This is my tangled world, her flirtatious glances, all night gangster flick marathons, mutual back massages, video recordings of Louis Farrakhan breaking down the hidden meaning of the world, holding her hand in the outdoor market as we shop for used books.

The last song on The Mis-education of Lauryn Hill ends. The room is silent.

Lauryn Hill is the earth mother goddess of Bob Marley's grandchildren. She sings about freedom and heartbreak, drops knowledge about the end of the millennium, praises Black Panther martyrs in a dope rhyme, stays manifesting knowledge, locks, head wraps, high water jeans and a cocoa butter voice in sold out stadiums and still keeps it real humble. In other words, she is the final word in any argument. And if you don't know that, then god, you need to get conscious and find out where you came from.

A slow hypnotic go-go beat starts, the bonus track. Lauryn's husky voice laps over us like a wave. Dani drums on the table with her hands. I start to sing the words that I have sung along to a thousand times in the past couple of months.

Raye says, "I want to play this at our wedding," and then she hits a tight hell fire and brimstone freestyle about devils, revolution and love.

The song ends.

"When all the computers and shit goes down, there is going to be war in the streets. They are going to make our hoods into martial law zones. They've already got impromptu checkpoints in the hood." Raye hugs herself. I imagine a baby, to replace the one she aborted last year, in her empty arms; Prince standing behind her, his green eyes looking at his star child. Their oil portrait, 'The Original Family', printed on a greeting card like the ones they sold at the conscious Black stores on 125th street.

"Yeah," Dani says, "but we have numbers on our side. People are finally going to have the power."

"Power to the people!" Raye thrusts her fist into the air.

"...to imagine a new world for themselves."

"We have to be prepared," I say. "Be ready. And know that we'll have to fight in order to survive."

Raye grabs my notebook and pen and opens to a fresh page. "We are going to need to start storing supplies. Food and water. Somewhere safe. And guns. I need to start a list. The year 2000 is less than a year away. It's a new day."

"Wait a minute," I say. "Where are we—no, how are we—going to get guns?"

Robin walks over to the CD player and switches CDs.

"Uh. uh. uh. Uh," the baddest bitch's voice groans over the speakers.

Raye walks back to the kitchen. "I fuck with some Lil Kim. Money. Power. Respect."

The air cracks like a record needle hit a scratch. The answer is obvious.

"Hey, Dani," I ask, "How much did you make dancing in clubs?"

"A lot more than I make now."

We could tip the balance.

We could be the spark for the revolution.

Raye turns to a clean page in the notebook. "I'll talk to Prince to see how much getting a couple of guns for us would cost. And we need to learn how to shoot properly. The Panthers took me to a gun range a few months ago. A gun is heavier than it looks."

She reaches above her door and pulls down the pistol.

"Dani you ever held a gun before?"

Dani shakes her head. Robin puts it on top of the notebook. We stare at its squat shadow marking an 'r' on the wide ruled paper.

I imagine myself a dark skinned Angela Davis, wearing a black cat suit, and timberland boots, a gun in one hand and a wad of cash in the other. I am hopping in and out of dark cars, dodging the feds, who are too afraid to come to my hood. I walk down the Brooklyn streets with no fear, because everyone knows I roll with the mariposas and nobody dares touch me.

"Well," Dani says stroking the gun, "I had better show you how to dance."

Lil Kim's raspy chants reach across the apartment like a clarion call to prayer.

Dani stands up and starts swinging her hips and her head, twirling around the tiny bed/living room. Raye and I get up and start dancing too, mouthing along with the music, and yelling out the chorus lines, slurring the words slightly. We circle each other, break away into our own rotations, and find each other again in the rhythms of the Brooklyn night. From the tiny window snow has started to fall again, and tomorrow anything could happen but right now in a basement studio apartment, we are warm and laughing and free, more powerful than any god.

BIRDS

Dena Rash Guzman

wish I could move like a bird,
flap my arms and remove the connection
between earth and assigned station

or just achieve the impossible:
open jars no one else can open,
make a colicky baby stop crying,
stave off the the apocalypse
with markers, cardboard and better spending habits,
be where you are when you need me

or be needed by you at all.

instead I flail, stunted,
pinwheeling my arms
like the last freak standing at the rave.
my heart is the end of days. It's a criminal foreclosure,
but never so hopeless
as an outer suburban strip mall.
It's not empty yet,
not collapsed or demolished

though it's less lofty than a bird
doing that thing birds do -

they let go. that's honest.

GOLD MINER PSALMS

Jenny Forrester

In the dream, there are ghosts and demons, saints and saviors, the archetypes we learn from and worship are geography, time and western American philosophy. The mesas stand guard against the world and the road is quiet and winding. I wake up from the dream path, falling from cliff edges and down into lonely valleys. I lift the curtain to check that the Milky Way is still there.

My kin, living and dead, plan for apocalypse – the Biblical one that hovers like an angry parent—threatening violence so you better mind.

But the apocalypse has already happened here.

The sage is what's left. I reach up and touch Jesus and his small crucifix on my wall.

My mom and brother dream that they were ancient Indians living not far from here.

"I was a woman holding a dying baby," my mom says.

My brother says, "I killed a deer with three arrows."

"You're never in the dream." My mom looks at me.

"Mine either." My brother says.

"Nope."

"Never."

We hike through the sage and red dirt looking for arrowheads. We find potshards, pieces of everyday life. Bone awls, needles, axe heads, stone tools for chipping away at pieces to make scrapers and knives.

There are times at the dinner table, when my mama says, "Save that for your brother." There's enough food so that we aren't truly hungry, but it's just enough. Sometimes I want more. I hate hearing, "Save that for your brother."

I want my mama to get food stamps. She won't. "I'm a Republican."

"But mom, it'd be so much easier. We wouldn't feel so sad about food."

"It's not right. None of us are starving. You could even lose some weight, you know."

"I know."

When we're out hunting for ancient western American treasure again, my mama picks up a potshard.

"If you're in charge of the food source, you are in charge."

A woman's world, full of in-charge women, passing craft and wealth on to the daughters while the men walked around, holding their bowls in front of them, begging for mercy and for food. Hunting from time to time, forced out of the village, to go freeze by desert fires to bring back only twenty percent of the total food supply.

My mama makes my world multi-layered.

Our high school is mostly white kids from families who don't have a lot of money and go to some kind of Christian church. We all understand that high school is to be the best four years of our lives. There are a dozen Native Americans. We say Indian.

Huey Whiteskunk has many brothers—Alvin, Galen, Jalen, and Waylen. Alvin is also Native American, taken later after his head was flattened a bit in a cradleboard, carried by a traditional mama. The authorities said it was abusive and wrong, like the teachers in our school who always pull Alvin into special ed even though he's as average as all the rest of us.

Galen, Jalen and Waylen are his Mormon brothers.

Galen's the most handsome. He's a football captain his senior year. He smiles a lot. He dies, in his forties, in an oil field, crushed in an accident.

Jalen's the biggest. He plays the line in football and doesn't smile. I'm afraid of him, even thought he never does anything to me.

My mom says that Huey was left at the hospital. She doesn't know the whole story, but she hears that his mother was an alcoholic and couldn't take care of Huey. He became a Mormon foster child.

Huey wears thick glasses, he's tall and thin, his thick black hair is cut short above his ears. He's quiet.

Huey is a junior. I'm a freshman.

A senior named Lori, who plays all three sports, cheer leads and in the summer rides barrel ponies in the rodeos, comes up to me, one day in the hallway at school, and says, "Huey wants to take you to the dance."

I don't know what to say. I'm afraid of her, but I don't need to answer. She turns to walk away, but turns around and says, "He's real sweet and if you hurt him, you'll be really sorry."

I tell him yes. I give him a note. He smiles and says, "I'll pick you up at your house."

Mom takes me out and buys me a new dress. I can't believe it. I don't get new clothes after the school year started. I don't want to take the dress off. I want to wear it until the dance.

The dance is a day or so after the bonfire–we burn a rival football player in effigy. We're allowed, this once, to dance on the gym floor. There's a strobe light and one of the Mormon boys is the D.J. because he has the best sound system.

Huey wears a powder-blue western style jacket with white piping, scorpion bolo tie, shiny cowboy boots. He picks me up at my trailer.

I wear a brown calico print of small red flowers. There's red piping along the yoke, western style. The ankle length skirt has a pretty flounce of an edge, more red piping, loose enough to poof out when I spin, but not enough to embarrass me.

My mom's happy that I'm going with him because it will be a first in our family. She doesn't mean any harm. She means for things to be set right, a race-relations do-over. She takes a picture while we stand side by side and try not to look at each other.

Huey is too shy to dance at Homecoming – except during the slow dances.

I'm too self-conscious to help him out. I can't make myself have so much fun that he has to jump in. So we sit there during all the fast dances. Uncomfortable and young in our western dress up clothes.

He drives me home in his Chevy pickup and is the perfect gentleman. I wave good-bye, but he peels out, frowning.

We never speak again just like we never spoke before the dance. We pass each other in the hallways, three or four times every day. We have small lives and small paths, but can't speak across that small hallway.

There are no concerts, no malls, no arcade places, nothing like that to entertain us. We live in a quiet world, loud only with gunfire, opinions and sermons and the music we play on our record players. There's a radio station for popular music and one for country and my brother and I don't listen to country music with few exceptions.

Our role models are the saints and saviors of western Colorado, for good or for ill with their good intentions and not.

The Sleeping Ute Mountain gives us some vision of a world where white families don't take Indian babies into their homes in the name of some religion, some misguided religious and cultural obligation. This earth-bound holy being counters the Latter Day Saint, Joseph Smith with his stories of saving Indians from themselves, those Lamanites, those rebels.

Mesa Verde, with its vast acres of juniper and piñon pine and abandoned cities filled with ghosts gives us bits of sandstone, ground to fine powder that cling to our clothes, cling to us. We'll smell sage and juniper in our skin until we die.

The La Plata Mountains stands like sentinels against the dry landscape and sustains us with rivers and stories of gold mines and makes us sturdier because of those winding roads and that mountain mythology, those stories of overcoming. We believe we can fly as we rise, from our 7,000 feet in elevation town, to the heights of the cliffs and peaks of Colorado.

The dark, starry skies give us stories, keep us connected to ancient things and to things larger than this small river valley. The quiet, cold nights whisper to us of tradition and loss, of change and timelessness.

The Sleeping Ute scares my brother, makes him a fighter, makes him feel protective, defensive. Someday, the mountain will rise and kill all the white people. I hear that mountain's rage, see his pain and believe that he can see that we aren't the destroyers, the kind of white people who hate. I hope that he sees through the thin veneer of our rose-white skin and the blue of our irises.

White people, here, believe that the emptiness of Mesa Verde means that all the real Indians are dead. I hear voices in that emptiness. I don't like some things that people say around here, but I want to belong. My family is small and scattered from far-away places, our ancestor's ghosts don't know where to rest.

Our mama is one of those people who doesn't belong to this place. She isn't afraid because she can leave whenever she wants. I know I have to leave, but I know that part of me will stay, the part that wants to belong here.

Huey graduates two years before I do. He smiles and smiles with his graduation cap. I watch him while he pushes the tassel to the other side.

Huey tries to kill himself, two years after that, by jumping off the two-story Mancos Hotel.

His Mormon foster family talks about Huey.

They say, "He's lost, confused. He's an alcoholic. He's ungrateful."

Not many years after that, Huey dies. And Alvin dies, too—young, not long after high school.

But maybe Huey doesn't die. Maybe he's a Skin Walker, a shape-changer, a powerful spirit. When he jumps off the motel, maybe he hits the ground because he's just learning to fly and because no one teaches him what's possible and nobody knows how to do the things that he's supposed to do.

My brother and I leave that small town when we grow up because there are people there that we don't want to become and it seems a near-impossible battle to overcome the flow of that particular hateful river. It's a town, like so many small towns with fewer than a thousand souls and miles between other small towns, where the world can start to feel like a lonely place and a person can start to feel like taking up more space to ease the burden of excess solitude. A person can feel like too much and can suffer a lack of perspective. Or a person can feel like too little and can suffer not feeling necessary and that can be dangerous. Cornered animals, cornered people and all that.

My brother and I return to the place – separately.

I return with my little daughter and take her to the places I love and take pictures of her with those expansive backdrops, feeling like I belong more, now, than I did before. My brother takes his sons and wife back there and they eat Navajo fry bread and his wife gets sick. His boys get a little sick, but they recover, as children will.

He says, "Guess you have to grow up with a certain kind of stomach."

And we laugh, thinking we're strong, like we have the anti-venom from being bitten by all those phantom rattler-saints. Like we have the story-cure, the gold-miner psalms and western mythology, deep in our brains keeping us strong and hopeful because we come from a place protected by guardian mountains and star-filled nights and people who still believe.

VOLITION

Colleen Rowley

We are a swampland—decomposition of what used to be. A layer of micro-organisms in a hue of purple. When you look into the swamp, our civilization of a hue fits nicely; looks as if we cared for a brief moment about how we could stand out from the rest of the swamp. Perhaps our purple may breed a new organism, far advanced from its birthing swampland.

We are a second...

a second...

...that has now passed.

THE END HAS COME, moved over us while we were still moving, for we are a fragment of a measurement so minute we have passed over our own death. Stuck in the beginning and the end. Too afraid to admit that although we are a hue of purple, we thirst for more. We set whatever stones we may have in hopes of crawling out of this swamp, out from our layer of self pity and greed, into one of confidence, into a race of moral giants driven by the metaphysics of ones self, driven by the unified subtle energy that runs through everything, driven by our own human possession of greatness.

SELF AS SAVIOR

C.

WHAT KIND OF RELIGIOUS GROUP DID YOU BELONG TO?
It was a community of devoted Christians who wished to recreate the ways of the New Testament church as described in the Bible. No formal name, due to the belief that the church was never named in the Bible—it was always named for its location, e.g. the Church in Rome...church was thought of as a natural, spiritual phenomenon that could occur when people came together in faith and spirit, and not an organization.

HOW OLD WERE YOU WHEN YOU JOINED? HOW LONG WERE YOU WITH THEM?
I was twenty-five. Nine years.

HOW DID YOU GET INVOLVED?
I was working part time for this crazy old charismatic Christian who took me to one of their meetings. He knew I was sort of floundering, awakening to my spirituality, seeking something more. He'd just discovered them and was excited about it all. I was curious, so I went. And it was lively and attractive and charismatic and very welcoming. I went back, got to know some of the people and felt some resonance. I stuck around and observed for a bit, then got drawn in and felt called to join them myself. Ironically the person who brought me never returned after I joined.

SO, WILL YOU TELL ME WHERE THIS TOOK PLACE?
Yes, this was Phoenix, Arizona.

IF YOU COULD DESCRIBE YOUR TIME WITH THEM IN ONE WORD, WHAT WOULD IT BE?

Intense.

DID THEY HAVE APOCALYPTIC IDEAS?

Yes, since everything was based in the Bible, and the Bible does describe an apocalypse, a collapse, a restructuring of the world. We expected apocalypse as an eventuality, perhaps in our lifetime, although we weren't certain when it would happen. And that the apocalypse would be a collectively self-determined event brought on by humanity's failure, or refusal, to acknowledge God's sovereignty over itself. It would predicate the return of God and godliness to the earth. And bring the end of the world as we know it. It was a goal. But I was living day-to-day and I honestly did not think about it much.

WHAT WAS THEIR SPECIFIC VISION OR PLAN FOR THE APOCALYPSE?

You know, I don't recall one. I think we expected to be "raptured" before anything major went down.

WHAT WAS THE GROUP'S OUTLOOK ON THE FUTURE OF HUMANITY?

That it was in jeopardy, on a downward spiral. But! Strangely we didn't go try and save anyone from this. There was a sort of "oh well," kind of spirit towards humanity around us, an "us and them" mentality. I see now that this was a bit elitist.

WHAT DID THEY THINK OF CIVILIZATION OR THE DOWNFALL OF CIVILIZATION?

That material civilization was fundamentally wicked, and that it should be avoided to maintain one's spiritual connection. A very black and white view. That downfall would be inevitable, and that humanity's failure or refusal to recognize God's sovereignty over us would inevitably bring this about.

WERE MEMBERS OF THE GROUP WHO WERE WILLING TO DIE FOR THE BELIEF SYSTEM?

Well, yes in theory. In 20th-century America, that's not really required, but we included the idea of martyrdom in our spiritual history. It was considered a high calling. I dug the romanticism of that, but it also frightened me.

HOW MUCH DID YOU HAVE TO SACRIFICE FOR THE GROUP AND/OR FOR THE RELIGIOUS TENETS?

I gave up all activities outside the church. Music, art, culture, friends, anything sourced outside the church. I didn't see a movie for nine years. I have a huge blank where the 90s should be, culturally, to this day. I also let go of many physical and emotional securities inherent in our American society. I moved a lot, lived with church families, in group homes. Gave up possessions, donated money. There's the concept of the "narrow way" set forth in the Bible as a path for a Christian pilgrim. The premise of giving up your life for the cause was built into the cause itself. It was part of the religious dynamic.

WHAT WAS THE MOST COMFORTABLE THING ABOUT THE RELIGIOUS GROUP?

The strong sense of community and family. There was an intense commonality that became very comfortable. We helped each other. It was a very large and tight family with a lot of unity. That part was beautiful.

WHAT WAS THE MOST DIFFICULT THING?

The letting go of so many physical and emotional anchors, without healthy replacements, placed us all into a certain head space, a sort of "group think" head space. It produced a vulnerability coupled with a bit of a crusader mentality, made everyone more dependent on the group than was wise for any of us. And there was a lot of feeling bad about yourself, always trying so hard and never quite making it.

WHY DID YOU LEAVE?

The tone and spirit became unbearably authoritarian for me. And some real inconsistencies surfaced between what was being taught and what was being lived and demonstrated by leadership versus what was expected from the rest of us. I began to see an undeniable chasm between the words and actions. Others saw it too, in fact there was a split down the middle of the group, from the top down, as a result. There had to have been hidden agendas there for a long time, because it all came on very quickly. It was still very, very difficult to leave, because I had burned every bridge behind me and had nothing to walk towards. I never want to do it again, but I learned so much about myself, about human nature, about truth and agendas and how systems go astray, how not thinking for yourself can be emotionally dangerous. It created in me a core conviction to never forfeit my critical thinking again.

WHAT WOULD HAVE HAPPENED TO YOU, IF YOU HAD STAYED?
Well for me, things got very strange spiritually and to stay, I would have had to forsake my core, my own true heart, my own mind, which I couldn't do. Physically, I would have likely remained single and donated the majority of my time to serving (working for free) as this was considered honorable.

WHAT ARE YOUR PLANS FOR THE FUTURE?
I'm not much of a planner. Right now I am focusing on creativity, on expanding the joy in my life.

WHAT WILL YOU DO IN CASE OF APOCALYPSE?
The truth is I will do nothing differently than I'm doing today.

WHEN THE SAVIORS ARE GONE

Leslie Gore

From the air, I see it all the way it was before we were here, and the way it will be when we are gone. I love a window seat. I take flying lessons in a superlight. A glider is the best, because it's so quiet, and I can feel the waves and thermals in the wind beneath the wings. I look down at all the squares and circles burned or fenced into the earth, and I know it will all be gone. Tract housing along false waterways, gone. Estuaries, man-made reservoirs, clear-cut patchwork, gone. The dams will fall, sub-stations go silent, and it will take the weeds exactly three months to topple every skyscraper in the world when all the paraquat runs out. Except in Dubai, and the sand will take care of that.

What I see, you don't want to know, but what would really make you uncomfortable is how happy I am when I see it. When we are gone! The trees will spread their succulent canopy and rejoice in breathing. Ocelots will multiply and solve the rodent problem in one generation. Dragonflies and birds of all colors will soar without fear of collision, or noise, or pollution. Butterflies will live longer than a day. The Canada geese will go back to migrating. Salmon will fill the streams and flying fish will eat up all the mosquitoes. The panthers and the bears that prowl North America will have plenty of elk and antelope eat, and a safe passage to their cousins in the north and south, roaming freely under crumbling freeways and across bridges. Condor and buffalo will thunder plains and sky. Bees will come out of hiding for a pollen revolution to revive the extinct. Dolphins and whales will sing their echoes into the deep, uninterrupted by our sonic terrorism. Giant squid will fear no capture, coral reefs regenerate, and the crashing waves will once more glow phosphorescent in the moonlight. No one will ever blow shit up on the bottom of the sea again – not on land, nor in space, and never on Mars.

All species, save us, even the rocks will be able to see all the stars at new moon. All of them. There will be no more confusion of circadian rhythms, no more hormone imbalance. The full moon, sung up by an assembly of wolves, will guide all tides, inner and outer, which will of course, by then, be one. Baboons will talk up a sunrise and scarabs roll in dung. All of the animals left will know when to step aside for an earthquake or a volcanic eruption, or a tidal wave, the way the sea gypsies did, and know how to be gracious about it. Maybe the sea gypsies will still be here. Maybe not. What if bigfoot and the yeti were finally able to come out? Would they start the whole thing over?

Here are my plans for the apocalypse: Get off big pharma, now. Eat only fresh, organic food. Learn to make own, custom medicine from plants grown in garden. Figure out acupuncture. Grow vanilla and cacao in a greenhouse. Make ice cream. Get a herd of cashmere goats, a silk-worm farm, and a share in a pristine oyster bed. Disengage from all corporate-owned media. Drink lots of clean, tested, spring or well water. Have as much sex as possible. Print books on a tabletop letterpress and bind in fine cloth or hand tooled leather. Write report back home to mother-ship about failed experiment. Love this earth until it breaks my heart to see me go. Love like there's no tomorrow.

Oh yes: and learn how to turn into a crow. This could come in handy.

CONTRIBUTORS

Lasara Allen lives in the Northern California outback without so much as a rifle to protect her family against the coming mayhem. When the hour comes, she will be hosting a "The First Day of the Rest of Your Life" retreat. Lasara is wife to her true love, and mother to two amazing young women.

Dani Burlison's latest preparation for the apocalypse is gleaning and canning food. When not co-editing a zine and teaching writing workshops with Petals and Bones, she writes for a Bay Area-based alt-weekly, *McSweeney's*, and a ton of other publications. She lives in Sonoma County with her kids, cats and chickens. www.daniburlison.com

H.A. Burton is a U.S. Army officer with seventeen years of experience in special operations, infantry, and engineering. He has taught Military Urban Operations and winter survival to Soldiers deploying to Iraq and Afghanistan, as well as foreign militaries, and is certified by the Federal Emergency Management Agency in the National Incident Management system and Incident Command. He lives with his wife and two kids in Portland, Oregon.

Yu-Han (Eugenia) Chao was born and grew up in Taipei, Taiwan. She received her MFA from Penn State and the Backwaters Press published her poetry book, *We Grow Old*, in 2008. For more writing and artwork, visit www.yuhanchao.com.

Roy Coughlin repairs washers and dryers for a living. In his spare time he lies about being a writer. His work has appeared at Smalldoggies Magazine and HOUSEFIRE. He does his best lying at expatdepot.blogspot.com.

Theresa J. Crawford is the mother of three wonderful daughters, and Bubbe to three delightful grandchildren. She is a writer and a psychotherapist with a private practice in Minneapolis.

Susan Davis directs undergraduate creative writing at University of California, Irvine. Poems have appeared in Cincinnati Review, Pequod and Alaska QR. Her book I Was Building Up To Something was released in 2011. Her poem *Farm Days* is installed in a public art project at the Lake June, Texas transit station.

Bonnie Ditlevsen can somehow always find the erotic amid the tragic, and the tragic amid the erotic. When not contemplating the marvelous notion of a searing diocryocin itch, she edits the Portland online literary magazine, *Penduline*, and writes memoir, poetry, noir fiction, and articles on education. www.pendulinepress.com

Katherine Ann Dreyfus grew up in Connecticut and now lives in Portland, Oregon with her daughter, her daughter's sneaky West Highland Terrier, and a devoted cat.

Golda Dwass moved to the Pacific Northwest from Chicago in 1991 to work with some friends in a nurse-midwifery practice. When the clinic closed in 2009, she started exploring her written voice. She lives in rural Southwest Washington on six acres with her husband. They have a large pottery studio, kilns, a huge garden, and one old dog—ready to live off of the grid.

Born in Cairo and raised in Kuwait, **Yasmin Elbaradie** currently resides in Seattle with her husband, two cats, and recently adopted puppy. She spends too much time playing phone Boggle.

Vickie Fernandez is an award-winning writer and alumni of Ariel Gore's Literary Kitchen. Her stories have appeared in many online publications including P*enduline Press, The Rumpus, Antique Children, Spurt Literary Journal, FYLM* and *Tiki Tiki*. She was the recipient of the 2011 Judith Stark award and a finalist in Hunger Mountain's 2010 competition for creative non-fiction. Vickie is currently working on a memoir while simultaneously wrangling a new set of unruly tales into submission.

Margaret Foley lives in Portland, Oregon. In moving from New Mexico to Oregon, she gave up steady access to sunshine and green chili for steady access to good coffee and winters without a lot of snow, which, most of the time, she considers a fair trade. If you'd like to read more of her writing, visit margaretfoley.com.

Jenny Forrester is so very grateful to everyone who submitted something to this anthology. Find more of her work at www.JennyForrester.com.

Margaret Elysia Garcia in accordance with her apocalyptic upbringing is hiding out in a cabin in the woods of the Sierra Nevadas waiting. Ironically, she is happily married with two children, three cats and a dog. Hopeful, even.

Ariel Gore is the creator of Hip Mama and the author of eight books including *Atlas of the Human Heart* and *All the Pretty People*. Find her in the kitchen at http://literarykitchen.com.

Robert Duncan Gray is an Englishman. He grew up in the Black Forrest of southwest Germany and graduated from the University of California, Santa Barbara, where he studied Art. He currently lives in Portland, Oregon, where he works with adults with developmental disabilities to produce a monthly television series called *FLASHtv* (www.FLASHtvPDX.com) and a weekly radio show called *the Full Life Radical Radio Show*. He is an editor for Housefire Publishing. More info at sillyrobchildish.com.

Dena Rash Guzman is a Las Vegas born author now residing on a 60-acre farm in the Mt. Hood Wilderness. She edits the literary journal *Unshod Quills.*

Derrick Jensen is an environmental activist and the author of 20 books.

Katie Kaput is a queer radical transsexual single mama writer with a survivalist history (and simple living present;). Her work has been published in a few anthologies (*Mamaphonic, It's a Boy!, Mamaphiles #4,* and the upcoming *This Bridge Called My Baby*). She is currently at work on both a novel and a collection of the first ten issues of her zine, *night cookies*. She blogs at http://nightcookies.wordpress.com and http://dispatchesfromtheragtag.blogspot.com.

Sarah Leamy is an internationally published writer, a professional clown, photographer, and performance artist. Her first novel *When No One's Looking*, published by Eloquent Books, came out in 2010. The book of travel stories, *Random Tales Out on the Road* and her second novel, *Lucky Shot*, both came out in 2011. Raised in England, she has made her home in Northern New Mexico. www.sleam.com

Kenna Lee line-dries clothes for herself and three children in northern California, blogs about school gardens (http://schoolgardenyear.blogspot.com/), and is slated to appear in a 2012 Women In Handcuffs calendar (activist real police cuffs, not bedroom cuffs, alas). Parts of this essay are adapted from her book, *A Million Tiny Things: One Mother's Desperate Search For Hope in a Changing Climate*, available through www.milliontinythings.com.

Lisa Loving is a news editor, talk radio host and disaster preparation hobbyist in Portland, Oregon. And yes, there really is a chain of volcanoes there.

Jolie Mandelbaum received her BA in Writing and Literature from the University of Pittsburgh and her MFA in Fiction Writing from American University. Her work has been featured in So to Speak and Calliope. She currently resides in Washington, DC, where she spends her time making trouble.

Tod McCoy is a technical writer in Seattle, Washington. He has been a Crazy 8s filmmaker semifinalist in Vancouver, BC, and attended the Clarion West workshop. His work has appeared on AntipodeanSF.com, Qarrtsiluni.com, and *The Gloaming* magazine. He is also the founder of Hydra House, a Pacific Northwest publisher of speculative fiction.

Brett Milligan is a practitioner, researcher, and educator and in the fields of landscape architecture and urbanism. He is the director of the collaborative research practice of Free Association Design based in Portland, Oregon.

Tomas Moniz edits and writes for ***Rad Dad*** http://raddadzine.blogspot.com/, loves zines, and lives with two amazing daughters, a bunch of chickens, bees, and a cat and dog in south Berkeley.

Linda Rand is a Portland artist and the proud mom of two boys, Harlan and Louis. Her favorite pastime is a late night philosophical talk with good company and red wine.

John Rodriguez' poetry appeared in the anthology ***One Word: Contemporary Writers on the Words They Love or Loathe*** and the journals ***PALABRA*** and ***Obscura***. He is a board member of Acentos Foundation, anassistant professor at Queensborough Community College/CUNY. He lives in The Bronx.

Colleen Rowley is a time traveling 80-year-old man, born again into the body of a small boy child with chubby freckled fingers. You won't look twice at her mustache.

Deb Scott is a therapist and writer living on the Washington side of the Columbia River Gorge. When she is not talking to people about their lives, she spends her time hanging out in coffee shops writing with other writing friends. (Okay, she talks and they try to write and she just hopes they will keep meeting with her anyway). Deb is working on a memoir about surviving her family history, writes poetry when she has no other choice, and is starting to believe that her childhood dream of 'being a writer' has actually always been true.

Carrie Seitzinger has been publishing and performing her poetry since 2004. Her first book of poetry, ***The Dots Don't Connect*** was self-published. She is a regular contributor and the poetry editor of ***Smalldoggies Magazine***, and co-hosts the monthly Smalldoggies Reading Series. She currently lives in Portland, Oregon with the prolific Matty Byloos, Patchen Seitzinger, and Parlsey "Sweet Sweet" Owens.

Evelyn Sharenov is a Portland, Oregon writer whose work has been published in numerous literary journals, ***Glimmer Train***, ***the New York Times***, as well as anthologies and Best American Short Stories. She has been awarded Oregon Literary Arts and Oregon Arts Commission grants. She is currently working on a novel, and a memoir in flash nonfiction pieces.

Sheri Simonsen works as a creative manager for a nonprofit organization in Seattle, Washington. Her writing projects have included stand-up comedy shows, musicals, and live memoirs. She plans on spending Earth's last year playing the ukulele and putting off yoga.

Kitty Torres takes the Metro North train to Manhattan most work days and while she rides she writes her life alive.

Mary Travers is the author of *Litany, A Novel*, available at Amazon.com and Barnes and Noble in both electronic book and paperback

Mai'a Williams, who should have been named Nikki' according to the poet Nikki Giovanni, is a visionary and media maker. She has lived and worked in the Middle East, southern Mexico and east Africa with refugee and displaced women under the threat of violence, also she has organized and accompanied communities and persons within the U.S./Canadian urban landscape, engaging in issues including: race, working poor, sex work, prisons, drug addiction, police brutality, and queer rights. Living in Cairo, Egypt, she is a freelance writer, poet, journalist, zinester, photographer, multi-media performer, and outlaw midwife.